The Pocket Picker

for Fine Art

Dear Sal + Vivian —

It was a pleasure
meeting you both. Hope
we can "Escher" in a great
New Year! ☺

Brook: Mahoy

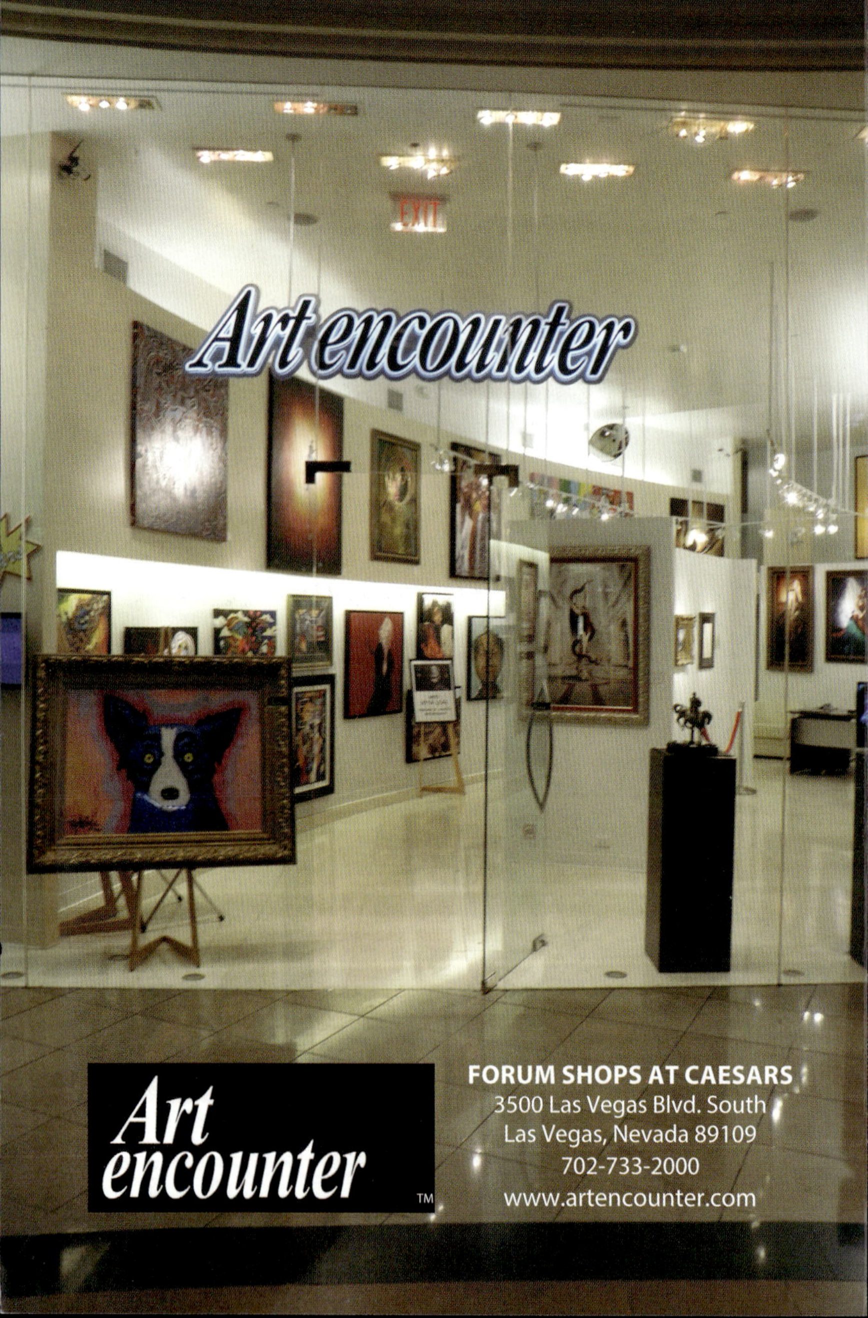
EXIT
Art encounter
Art encounter™
FORUM SHOPS AT CAESARS
3500 Las Vegas Blvd. South
Las Vegas, Nevada 89109
702-733-2000
www.artencounter.com

The Pocket Picker

for Fine Art

A Field Guide to Procuring and Profiting in Fine Art

Brett K. Maly

The Pocket Picker: For Fine Art
A Field Guide to Procuring and Profiting in Fine Art

Copyright ©2014, Brett K. Maly

Published by:
    Bear N Desert, LLC
    Las Vegas, Nevada

Library of Congress Control Number: 2014904459
ISBN: 978-0-9915380-0-3
$16.95US

The majority of artworks photographed in this text are available for purchase. To inquire, please call the offices of *Art encounter*, 702-227-0220.

Dedication

I would like to thank my loving family: My Father, Rod (the best "illiterary agent" a son could ask for); my Mother, Kristine (and my A #1 editor); my wife, Anna (whose encouragement kept me moving forward), and my children, Jocelyn and Russell (who let me out of countless Lego and Lincoln Log sessions to write).

I'd also like to thank William Gregory and Matt Sattel for their friendship, artistic expertise and graphic assistance; Jim Petty for his enthusiasm and publishing assistance; Pawn Stars for their continued support, and the professional staff of *Art encounter*, whose nearly twenty-five year track record of excellence in the art world has helped to make me look good!

Table of Contents

Foreword

After twenty-five years in the business, I may never know what's going to come through my door ... but I do know fine art is becoming a bigger part of it. Purchasing fine artworks for investment, while potentially lucrative, is not for the uninitiated. In my years of buying and selling I have learned many lessons—often the hard way—and now pride myself on developing a considerable storehouse of personal knowledge about the art world and the artists that inhabit it.

Despite this, there are times I'm presented with unknown works, or have questions about an intriguing piece I may be inclined to buy. During those times, I always get the best advice I can find. For the past four years, Brett has been my "art guy" for Gold and Silver Pawn Shop fine art purchases. Whenever I need authentication, valuation, or simply a second opinion, my first call is always to Brett. With his over 20 years of experience in art, I know I can trust his judgment and counsel.

The Pocket Picker: For Fine Art will provide you much of the same expert information Brett gives me to help make the crucial decisions to either buy or pass. Whether you are a novice or expert, *The Pocket Picker: For Fine Art* will give you an excellent quick reference source that will help you to make the most of your purchases.

—Rick Harrison, PAWN STARS

Introduction
(Picking's Popularity)

Over the last few years, my business as an art appraiser has shifted away from the evaluation of stuffy estate collections, and towards works brought in by individuals who, for reasons economic and social (Pawn Stars, anyone?), have turned to garage sales, swap meets, antique malls, thrift stores—even their own attics—looking for buried treasures. In addition to being fun—who hasn't played pirate as a kid, pursuing the "X" marking the spot?—it can prove lucrative. In 2009, two paintings by Peruvian artist, Federico del Campo, were discovered in a Toronto Goodwill. They sold for $134,000. In 2010, photographic negatives purchased at a California garage sale were attributed to renowned Yosemite photographer, Ansel Adams. They were valued at $200 million!

I've enjoyed the trend as well. Rather than appraising traditional gallery artworks with established provenance and authenticity, more and more often I find myself confronted with blank canvases. Not literally, of course, but often a familiar style and (if I'm lucky) a partial signature are all I have to divine a painting's history and potential value. Nothing is more gratifying to me, personally, than identifying an unknown work and assigning it a tangible value based on extrapolated value characteristics. (When I wasn't playing pirate as a kid, I was playing detective!) Informing clients of my discoveries—as I did with two watercolors by Marie Laurencin, purchased for their frames at a garage sale—is an added bonus.

It isn't always good news, however. More often than not, there's a reason these "treasures" have been abandoned in thrift stores or sold at garage sales. That's where *The Pocket Picker* comes in. Consider it your Field Manual for the procurement of fine art.

Though it's specifically catered to those who want a ready reference guide for spontaneous purchases, much of the information is applicable to the big picture as well. By "big picture" I'm not referring to that giant painting over the sofa (at least, not necessarily), but rather an overall enhancement of your knowledge and enjoyment of fine art in any setting.

I hope you enjoy *The Pocket Picker*. Even more importantly, I hope it helps you to tell the difference between a pitiful poster and a priceless Picasso.

Problems with Picking

Have you heard the story about ex-truck driver, Teri Horton, who found an alleged Jackson Pollock painting at a California thrift shop in the early 1990s? She appeared with the painting on "The Montel Williams Show," "The Tonight Show" with Jay Leno, and the "Late Show with David Letterman," and her story was subsequently made into a movie entitled *Who the $&% is Jackson Pollock*? Her rough-around-the-edges persona juxtaposed against the hoity-toity art world made for good viewing; however, twenty years after her discovery, the work, despite having been examined by everyone from Pollock scholars to Police forensic experts, has still not been authenticated or sold.

I tell you that not to discourage you, but to make you aware of the pitfalls of purchasing fine art through unorthodox locations like estate sales and antique shops. Art sold through a fine art gallery will be well-displayed, well-lit, and well known to the people selling it. You'll be lucky if art sold at a swap meet has a price tag. Art from a gallery typically comes with some sort of guarantee. Art from a flea market typically comes with bugs.

Beneath the layers of dirt, however, these framed mysteries were once shiny and new. They once sat on an artist's easel as he proudly added the final brushstrokes. They once hung in the spotlight on a gallery wall. And they were once purchased by someone excited to be in the presence of their beauty. As a picker, you don't need to be a humanitarian for abandoned artwork, but you need to recognize the ones worth saving.

By the time you've finished *The Pocket Picker*, you will. Not only will you be prepared to deal with the unique challenges of picking, but you'll also be able to do the one thing that any successful picker needs to do: take advantage of other people's ignorance. That sounds horrible, doesn't it? (I didn't even like writing it.) The truth is, however, if everyone knew exactly what they had and its true value, pickers probably couldn't exist. If you make a great find in the field, chances are it's only because someone else missed it.

Picking Professionally

Beauty is in the eye of the beholder. It's an old cliché, but it's true. In the retail art business, I always encourage my clients to buy what they like. It doesn't matter if the work is a painting or a poster, if you enjoy looking at it on your wall and it brings joy and beauty into your life, then it was a worthwhile purchase.

However, that's not what this book is for. You don't need me to tell you what you like, and I presume you didn't buy this book in order to help you find a painting for over your sofa. You're looking to find value as a picker and, no matter what your thoughts are of Picasso as an artist, you're not going to turn your nose up at one of his paintings should it appear at a local estate sale.

For the purpose of this book we will be focusing on fine art over decorative art. Definitions vary, but I personally classify fine art as exclusive artworks (such as originals or limited editions) by established or listed artists renowned for more than simply creating aesthetically pleasing wall-filler. By contrast, decorative art is something created or manufactured purely for its ornamentation. There's nothing wrong with that, and all art will have some value, but you're not going to make your fortune picking posters or mass-produced oil paintings from China.

With that in mind, there are certain rules in the fine art world that you should be aware of. Knowledge and utilization of these rules separates good art from bad art, and talented artists from amateurs. Since you'll be interested in the former (bad art by amateur artists is no way to make money), you'll want to have a general understanding of what constitutes good art. Some artists, like our aforementioned friend Picasso, may routinely break the rules, but it comes from a desire to challenge convention, not ignore it. As Pablo himself once said, "It took me four years to paint like Raphael, but a lifetime to paint like a child."

In the back of this book, you'll find a glossary with short definitions of important artistic terms, processes and stylistic movements in the art world. (**I have underlined glossary words in the text for easy reference**.) I recommend perusing them and developing a general understanding of how they apply to individual pieces of art. Practice evaluating the artwork on your own walls. Does the piece feature a balanced <u>composition</u>? Are items in proper <u>perspective</u>? Is it rendered <u>realistically</u> or <u>impressionistically</u>? You don't need to become a professional art critic, but the faster you develop a critical eye as a picker, the more time and money you'll save yourself.

Once you feel familiar with the terms, visit a few <u>galleries</u> and <u>museums</u>, and maybe even take an art appreciation class or two. Art should be experienced in person. Good art will evoke feeling and emotion, and the more art you see, the better you'll be able to understand why. For each piece, take into account the work's context and the artist's intent. Nearly all of Jackson Pollock's artwork can be classified as "<u>Expressionist</u>," but was that expression born of anger, in fits of gestural color? Or was it thoughtfully composed in rhythmical and soothing patterns? Why did Diego Rivera make his background figures larger than foreground objects? Was it because he was lousy at <u>perspective</u>? Or did it stem from a desire to draw attention to a specific subject, such as a toiling farmer, within a busy <u>com-</u>

<u>position</u>? Experience is the best teacher. The more art you see, the more confident you'll be when confronted with a mystery artwork at your local antiques mall.

Once you feel prepared to venture from the bright lights and <u>provenance</u> placarded safety of <u>museums</u>, it's time to gather your …

Picking Paraphernalia

Any tradesman needs the proper tools to succeed and picking is no exception. The good news is, you probably have most of what you'll need in your possession already. I don't think you'll need (or want) to carry a briefcase for every excursion; however, you'll want to keep the following items handy:

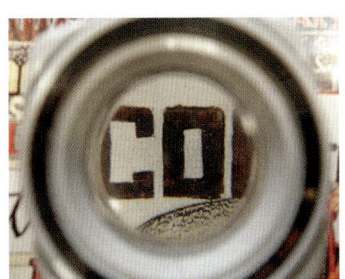

Magnifying Glass: This is my number one tool. It has innumerable uses—from identifying print types, to verifying signatures and analyzing condition. You'll want one with at least 5x magnification.

A good magnifying glass should be the first tool in your tool box.

Pad and Pen: Don't trust your memory if you plan to do additional research on a particular item. Take notes about all known facets of the piece: composition, materials, size, artist's name, inscriptions, markings and any other identifying features.

Camera: See "pad and pen." Cameras may not be usable in all situations, as some businesses frown on pictures being taken in their establishment. Always ask permission (or forgiveness!).

Gloves: I recommend having two pairs: 100% cotton for examining and handling of paintings and <u>prints</u> on paper, and sturdy workman gloves for moving <u>sculpture</u> or art in frames. Oils in our fingers and hands can stain artwork over time, and our nails can cause abrasions to delicate surfaces. When moving framed art, you can worry less about damaging the art … and more about the art damaging you. Over the years, I've been cut by jagged glass, stabbed by rusty hanging wires, and removed more splinters than I can count. Be careful!

Tape Measure: Size matters in the art world. In addition to being a crucial value characteristic for <u>original</u> art, it can be useful for authenticating prints. For example, original prints by an artist may have been issued in one size, while posthumous reprints or forgeries may be another.

Small Flashlight or Penlight: Have you been to a well-lit thrift store? Didn't think so.

Cellular or Smart Phone: From inquiring to regional businesses about their hours and selection while on the road, to "Googling" an artist's name while on location (or phoning a friend to do so if your phone is as old as mine), a cell phone is a must for the practical picker. Besides, how else are you going to call home to brag about your latest find?

Laptop Computer: This is optional, and I'll admit that I don't even own one, but it's a useful tool for taking notes and storing reference materials (like this book!) for easy access.

Cash: Although most places outside of garage sales take credit now, you'll always get more bang for your buck with cash. Don't leave home without it.

Now that you've got your bags packed it's time to decide on the best ...

Places to Pick

The world is your oyster! Ok, maybe not quite, but life in the 21st Century allows for nearly pole-to-pole coverage through e-mail, Internet, and cheap long distance telephone rates. Unfortunately, this deeper pool of resources allows for more sharks and barracudas. By the time you're done with this manual, you'll be better equipped to deal with them, but for now let's concentrate on where to fish.

Picking opportunities are everywhere—from galleries to garages. Don't assume a particular resource is too snooty or too trashy to offer value. However, as a picker you'll want to concentrate most heavily on outlets that provide the best combination of opportunity and investment return. Here are ones to consider:

Estate Sales

Estates are being liquidated all the time—it's just a matter of finding them. The Classifieds section of the paper used to be the go-to, but now various online resources are available for discovering and previewing them. Estatesales.net, for example, will let you search estate sales by area and even e-mail you when a sale is in your neck of the woods.

Take advantage of any online previews. You don't want to waste a Saturday afternoon traveling across town for an estate in which the prized possession is a collection of vintage Happy Meal toys. Online previews are typically (and often intentionally) vague, but they will give you an idea of the scope of the collection and how many art items will be featured. As an appraiser, context is important and it should be for you, too. An unknown painting in a home with nice china and antique furniture is more intriguing than one in a home full of videogames and beanbag chairs. If an online preview isn't available, try to call someone to find out a little more about the estate and its featured items.

Garage Sales

Drive around a neighborhood early on a Saturday and, chances are, you'll find cardboard boxes with Sharpee-drawn arrows pointing you toward your next picking opportunity. As with Estate Sales, the key is making efficient use of your time. Look for ones advertised online or in your local paper. Many neighborhoods, especially those governed by a Home Owner's Association or similar entity, have neighborhood-wide garage sales at particular times of the year. These can provide a target rich environment full of rich targets. Take advantage.

And be sure to set your alarm! Don't expect a 200 year-old

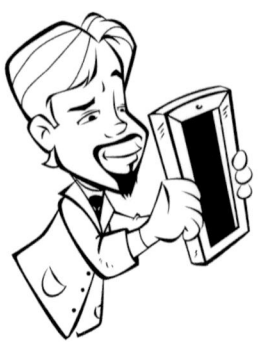

Brett Says:
"Remember, the early bird gets the Worms. Maybe even Jules Worms, a prominent 19th Century French artist!"

oil painting to still be resting next to that broken lawnmower by 10 a.m., so hit the road at dawn. If you find yourself at the garage sale of a nice estate with no artwork being shown, ask if they have any they'd like to sell. Some people may not feel comfortable setting that glass-covered <u>etching</u> on the floor of their garage, but would be more than happy to bring it out for you to see.

Auctions

No, not Sotheby's or Christie's, where rich Europeans in Armani suits bid against Billionaires from Dubai. I'm talking about local charity and "for profit" auctions, where you can bid on everything from homemade gun racks to taxidermied badgers. Most items put up at these auctions are either from estates or from private collectors looking for quick cash. They're rarely "specialized" (i.e. art, jewelry, coins, etc.), which can be both good and bad. It's good because it increases the chance of valuable items slipping through the cracks, but bad because it means there will be a lot of sifting through items in which you may have no interest.

Like estate sales, make sure you preview the items. Most auctions will have a preview period in the days or hours leading up to it. If you're not allowed to personally inspect an item, or don't get the chance prior to bidding, you're probably better off passing. Another thing to remember is that many <u>auction houses</u> employ "shills": in-house bidders who drive-up the prices of certain items. A shill bidding on an item is a clear indication that the auction house and auctioneer are fully aware of a piece's value and don't intend for it to be sold cheaply. It's doubtful you'll get a good price, at least from a picking per-spective, if you find yourself bidding against a shill.

Online

Nowadays, you can preview, bid on, and purchase items from around the globe with a few clicks of the mouse. This convenience comes with a price, however. Physical inspection of online items isn't typically available until after purchase, and the anonymity of online transactions makes it fertile ground for unscrupulous sellers. As an appraiser, I typically refuse ap-praisal assignments where physical inspection is impossible and, as a picker, you should adopt a similarly cautious philos-ophy. There is danger in trusting your money and livelihood to poor jpeg photos and someone else's "expertise." Trust your own judgment, not that of an elderly woman in Poughkeepsie who claims to have a rare Marc Chagall.

While I'm not a big proponent of purchasing art online, good value can be had if you know what you're looking for. For example, I've known several people who made lucrative on-line purchases of artworks that were misidentified by the sell-er because the signature was illegible. (Note to self: watch for eBay paintings attributed to "Jackson Tollock.") Just make sure there is some sort of return policy if the work fails to match its description.

Antique Malls/Thrift Stores/Consignment Shops

These typically aren't great venues for picking fine art. First of all, most of these locations are dingy and jam-packed with items, making it difficult to walk, much less examine something properly. The flashlight/penlight in your tool kit (see page 10) will help, but it may not be enough to insure an art item's pertinent value characteristics. Ask if a work can be moved to better light, or taken outside for inspection. If you're in the dark on an artwork, literally and figuratively, you're probably better off passing.

Secondly, it's a crapshoot as to what will be there. Good stuff will likely be snatched-up quickly, while junk will sit for months. To counter this, befriend the proprietor and ask them to contact you when they get art in. Any disadvantage alerting them to the fact that you're a collector is far outweighed by having first dibs.

Art Galleries

This is not fertile ground for the traditional picker, who is looking to get a great deal at the expense of an unwitting or desperate seller. Most galleries know what they're selling and its value. However, as you grow from an "art picker" to an "art collector" (as I hope you do) you'll want to consider galleries. You probably won't make a purchase at a <u>gallery</u> that will get your name in the paper, but good value can still be had, especially if you get in on the ground floor with a promising emerging artist, or understand the market for an established one.

Picking and Choosing
(What You'll Be Picking From)

Art dates back to the cave <u>drawings</u> of early man and extends to the digital art and <u>prints</u> of today. In between, there have been millions of artists and thousands of ways to produce art. While I doubt you'll be confronted with any cave drawings during your picking excursions, you'll probably be confronted with a lot of the "in between."

When you first begin picking, most pieces will look promising. Over time, most pieces will begin to look like junk. THAT'S when you know you've arrived! Because unless you plan on going broke quickly, you'll want to pass over the vast majority of what you see. As I mentioned in the introduction, there's generally a good reason why artwork ends up at Farley's Flea Market. It could be its horrible condition, or the fact that it's a mass-produced <u>lithograph</u>, or it could just be lousy (or all three in one!). Regardless, you'll want to spend as little time and money on this junk as possible.

Since separating the wheat from the chaff is the key to any successful picker, I've devised the Value Pyramid (pages 22-23) to assist you in the ranking of artwork you discover.

These rankings are dictated by quality and artist involvement in the process. <u>Oil</u> paintings on <u>canvas</u>, in addition to being in color and easier to preserve, require more proficiency and preparation than a simple pencil <u>sketch</u> on paper. Similarly, <u>etchings</u> and <u>woodblock</u> prints typically require an artist to create the original <u>block</u> or <u>plate</u> from which the artwork is derived, whereas <u>offset lithographs</u> are mass-produced from a photographic process in which the artist may or may not have any involvement at all.

Obviously, this pyramid is contingent upon all things being equal—a signed and numbered Matisse <u>lithograph</u> is going to be worth far more than an <u>original</u> painting by your local art fair participant—however, this will give you an idea of the desirability of particular artistic media among collectors and connoisseurs.

Original, one-of-a-kind artworks

At the top of the value pyramid, colored red, are individual creations by a single artist. They weren't printed or mass-produced by machinery—they were hand-crafted by the artist with (we hope) pride, attention and care. For that reason, original works are generally considered the most rare and desirable of all artworks.

However, not all originals are considered equal. That <u>watercolor</u> on paper may be just as well-composed by the artist as one of their <u>oils</u> on <u>canvas</u>, but with few exceptions, will not achieve the same value. Fair or not, there is a clear delineation of value in original art based on the materials used.

Oils/Acrylics on Canvas/Board

<u>Oil</u> paintings on <u>canvas</u> or board will typically achieve the highest value of any artistic media. There are a number of reasons for this, but the primary reason is that it was the preferred technique of most Masters and, factual or not, perceived to require more expertise.

Acrylics didn't come into vogue as a mainstream artistic media until the second half of the 20th century. Since they were less expensive and dried much quicker than oils, they quickly became popular among recreational and emerging artists—further enhancing the prestige of oils as a media for professionals.

You're probably wondering, then, why I lumped acrylics in the same Value Tier as oils. The answer's simple: You probably won't be able to tell the difference. There are ways—oils can have a distinctive odor, while acrylics sometimes have a plastic appearance—but in the field you'll have bigger issues to worry about. In my experience, the disparity in values between oils and acrylics by recognized Post-War artists is minimal.

Identifying oils and acrylics on canvas or board is usually a pretty simple process. They generally will not be under glass—paintings need to "breathe" (sometimes for several years) in order for the materials to fully dry, cure and bond, and covering an oil or acrylic painting with glass also threatens its impasto (surface texture). As a result, you should be able to inspect the painting's surface closely. On an original oil or acrylic you'll see brushstrokes and/or texture throughout the composition.

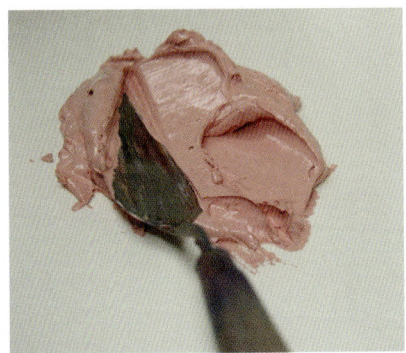

IMPASTO is the surface texture of an artwork. This will be visible on original oil and acrylic paintings. Impasto may be heavy, if applied with a palette knife (left), or subtle if applied with a fine brush.

Value Pyramid

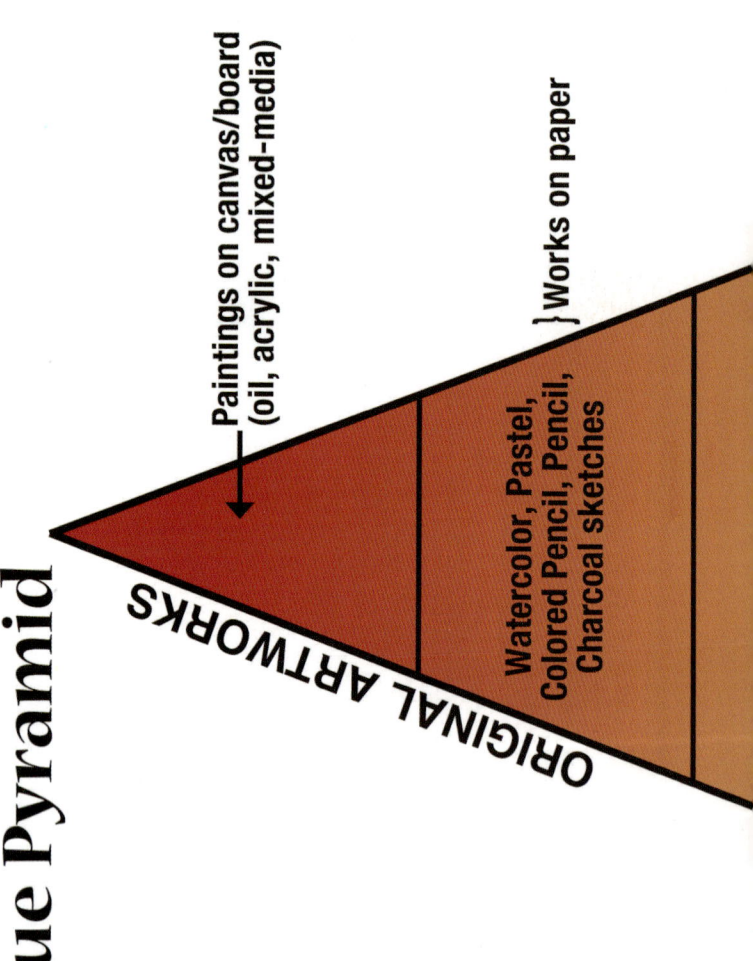

ORIGINAL ARTWORKS

Paintings on canvas/board
(oil, acrylic, mixed-media)

Watercolor, Pastel,
Colored Pencil, Pencil,
Charcoal sketches

} Works on paper

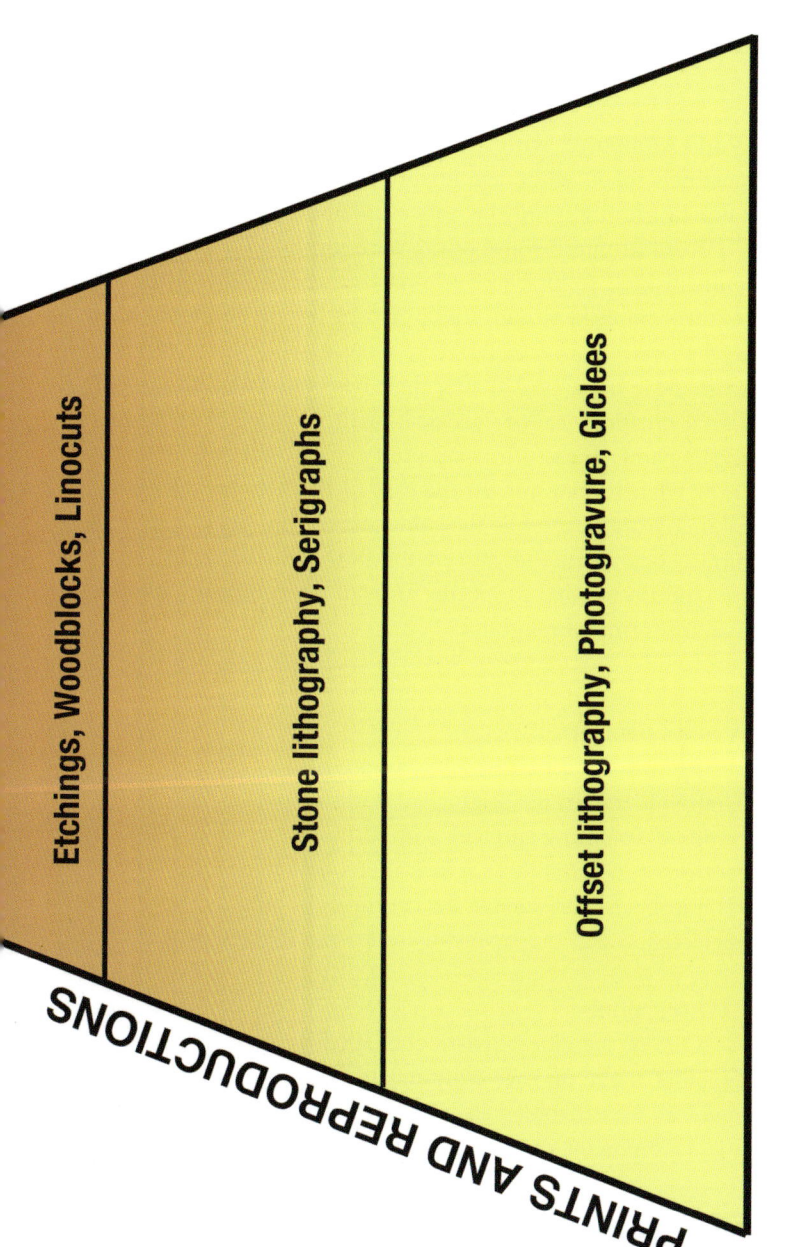

PRINTS AND REPRODUCTIONS

Etchings, Woodblocks, Linocuts

Stone lithography, Serigraphs

Offset lithography, Photogravure, Giclees

Works composed with a palette knife could have impasto a half-inch thick, while the texture on a work composed with a fine brush might only be noticeable upon close inspection.

Keep in mind, some <u>prints</u> were produced on <u>canvas</u> and "<u>embellished</u>" to look like <u>originals</u>. In the middle of the 20th century, publishers and studio artists began dolloping clear <u>acrylic</u> over prints transferred to canvas, while more recently, artists have begun enhancing their own canvas prints (usually digital creations called "<u>giclees</u>") with areas of hand-applied acrylic paint. These prints are pretty easy to identify once you know what to look for. In the case of the former, the embellishments are clear while the color comes from the <u>lithographic</u> surface below. In the case of the latter, the embellishments are typically applied to specific areas of the <u>composition</u> rather than uniformly throughout.

Works on Paper

Just below <u>oils</u> and <u>acrylics</u> on <u>canvas</u> or board on the value pyramid hierarchy are <u>original</u> artworks on paper. An artwork's "<u>support</u>" (painting surface) is important to its value primarily because of its durability, or lack thereof. While works on canvas and board can survive for centuries as long as they're not neglected, works on paper can erode even if given proper care.

1. Watercolors

One of the oldest artistic media (there is evidence of <u>watercolors</u>' usage on cave paintings in Paleolithic Europe), watercolors were dabbled in by most Masters (Albrecht Durer was a proponent of the media during the Renaissance). Be-

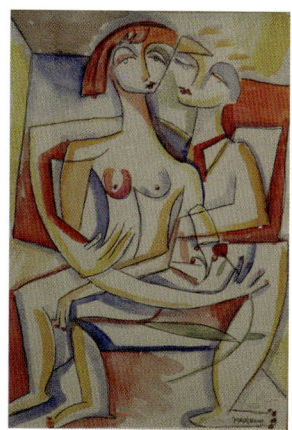

"He Loves Me."
Watercolor by Jennifer Main.

cause of this, and the fact that watercolors are a challenging media to master, they typically top the value hierarchy for works on paper.

Watercolors appear transparent upon inspection, and the colors typically appear luminous because individual pigments are laid on the paper in a pure form, with few fillers to obscure them. In most cases, watercolors produce a natural wrinkling in the paper as they dry. The extent of this puckering effect varies with the quality of paper and its treatment, but is usually visible upon close inspection.

Despite their distinctive appearance, watercolors are often difficult to identify in the field. Unlike oils and acrylics, they are usually presented under glass, making close inspection challenging. Additionally, certain types of prints, such as woodblocks and stone lithography, can create images with similar transparency and feel. Fortunately, most printing techniques produce their own distinctive trademarks and, once you're familiar with them, the media can be divined through the process of elimination.

2. Pastels

Pastels, like watercolors, were utilized by many Masters from the Renaissance on (they were first referenced by Leonardo da Vinci). Pastel <u>drawings</u> by artists renowned for their usage, such as Pierre Auguste Renoir, have sold for millions of dollars. In most cases, however, their ceiling of value is limited, at least in relation to comparably sized <u>oils</u> and <u>acrylics</u>, because of their delicate nature and perception of being for <u>sketches</u> rather than polished studio <u>compositions</u>.

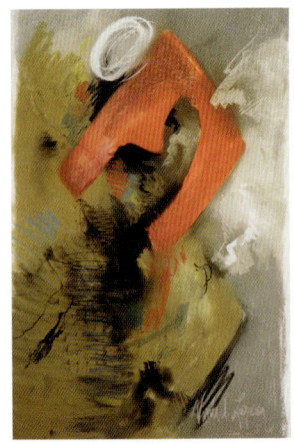

"Contemplating Mona Lisa."
Pastel by Vance Larson.

For identification purposes, <u>pastels</u> typically appear even more luminescent than watercolors, as they are composed strictly from pure pigment and an inert binding material. (Impressionists, in particular, loved the <u>medium</u>, as it enabled them to capture the movement, energy and light play so crucial to the style.) Unlike <u>acrylics</u> and <u>oils</u>, which feature texture and brush marks, and <u>watercolors</u>, which are transparent, pastels will ap-

Please Note:
Although I've ranked pastels below watercolors on the Value Pyramid, values for pastels can far exceed the values met for comparably-sized watercolors, especially in the hands of a master (Renoir and Degas, for example, found pastels preferable for their unique brand of Impressionism); however, the general perception that watercolors are more challenging than pastels frequently tips the value battle in their favor.

pear smooth and velvety on the paper. <u>Pastels</u> can be easily smudged and disturbed, which lowers their value ceiling in relation to other media, but can help you to identify them in the field. Pawn shops, flea markets, and swap meets aren't known for their gentle treatment of fine art, so there's a good chance you'll find loose pastel dust on the work's surface or trapped within its framing. Look for particles stuck to the inside of the glass (static electricity often causes loose dust to "jump" onto its surface) or settling around the base of the matting. Smudging, evident as a blurring of the image, may also be visible at particular points within the composition.

3. Crayon/Colored Pencil

Typically, the more modern the materials, the less value they'll have in the eyes of collectors. Leonardo da Vinci might

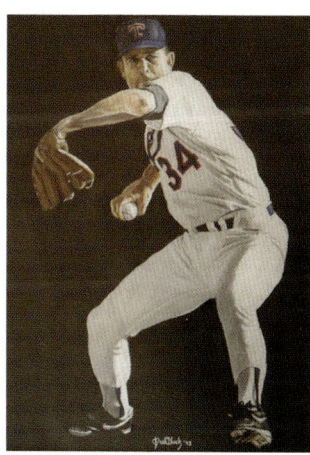

"Nolan Ryan."
Colored pencil by Dean Huck.

have played around with watercolors and pastels, but could you picture him with a box of Crayola? Twentieth Century masters like Picasso, who experimented with just about every artistic media in his ninety-one years, have softened the stigma against the use of supposedly amateurish materials like these, but their values will still pale against more established and historical media.

<u>Crayons</u> are similar to pastels in appearance; however,

their waxy nature limits blending and shading, so colors will appear even more luminescent and uniform. They won't have a <u>pastel's</u> signature "dust," but are identifiable in other ways. Crayons sit heavy on paper, obscuring its natural texture and weave, and unlike pastel, which lies flat on the <u>support</u>, have a texture that is noticeable upon close inspection. <u>Crayons</u> don't apply very evenly, so you'll see variations in the thickness of texture and line.

Colored pencil lies flat on paper, but since it is a hard media applied with a sharp point, is identifiable by its sketch-like lines. Depending on the amount of pressure used, indentations in the paper may also be noticeable (especially where the colors are darkest and most heavily applied).

4. Pencil/Charcoal/Pen and Ink

There's a reason you don't see too many black and white movies being made anymore. In the art world, just like in the cinema, color is king. It's considered to be more visually stimulating and, therefore, is usually more desirable. Occasionally, as with 2012's Oscar winning, and appropriately titled film, "The Artist," an absence of color is a stylistic choice that resonates with the viewer and enhances a work's value ("Guernica," Picasso's bloodless depiction of a bloody battle, is an example from the fine art world); however, this is the exception rather than the rule.

For identification purposes, compare charcoal with <u>pastel</u> and pencil with colored pencil. Pen and ink, as with <u>watercolor</u>, is difficult to identify in the field, as certain printing techniques, especially <u>block</u> printing, can mirror its effects. As with watercolor, the best bet is to become familiar with the different

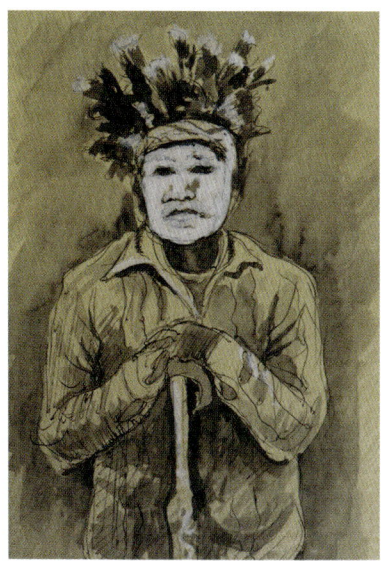

"Medicine Man."
Pen and ink. Artist unknown.

printing processes and their own identifying characteristics.

As I'm sure you've surmised, this list is far from comprehensive— artists have painted with everything from egg yolk to blood—but it represents the media you are most likely to be confronted with as a picker. Keep in mind, many artists utilize a mixture of media in their <u>originals</u>. (Termed, cleverly, "mixed-media" art) Once you can identify the media and <u>support</u> used, you should be able to rank the work within the value pyramid based on their combination. For example, a colored pencil on paper enhanced

Please Note:
You won't see oils and acrylics on paper that often. Unless properly sealed, the paper wrinkles and its porousness interferes with the paint's ability to cure; however, if you do find an oil or acrylic on paper, and it appears in good condition, bump it to the top of the Value Pyramid for originals on paper.

with watercolor will likely have more value than a charcoal sketch, but less value than an acrylic with collage on canvas.

Prints and Reproductions

The bottom half of the pyramid, colored in yellow, is where we'll find prints and reproductions. Original paintings by respected artists have been collectible for centuries; however, the collection of prints for anything other than filling walls is a relatively recent phenomenon. The printing of artwork began in the 15th Century with woodcuts and metal engravings, and although it quickly became popular with artists and patrons alike (it enabled artists to expand the audience for their work, while it enabled the public to see famous art in the days before photography and mass tourism), it wasn't until the 20th century that the production and collection of fine art prints became its own cottage industry.

As with media used in the creation of one-of-a-kind art, the methods and types of printmaking are plentiful. Some techniques require a tremendous amount of attention from the artist in the process, and the final product can be just as unique as an oil on canvas, while other processes are more mechanical, requiring little more than a flip of a switch to produce reproductions by the thousands. As a result, prints have a value spectrum nearly as wide as that for one-of-a-kind artistic creations. A rare etching of Albrecht Durer's *"Knight, Death and the Devil"* (which I evaluated for **Pawn Stars**) can sell for hundreds of thousands of dollars, while an offset lithograph of the exact same scene sells for $10!

If that weren't confusing enough for the profiteering picker, identifying types of <u>prints</u> can be difficult. In the field, most prints will be framed and under glass, making close inspection impossible. (Business owners generally frown on their merchandise being taken apart prior to purchase.) This can be especially problematic since a <u>print's</u> condition is usually tied to its value. That 16th Century Japanese <u>woodblock</u> could be worth a pretty penny in <u>mint condition</u> … but not if it's been trimmed to fit the frame and glued onto the matting.

Add to this the overall volatility of the print market (values are particularly susceptible to economic factors and stylistic trends), and you'd be forgiven if you think it might be best to forgo the picking of prints entirely. You'd be wrong, however. In fact, it is because of these pitfalls that the picking of prints can be extremely lucrative. Most people can identify a painted work on canvas, but few can tell the difference between a <u>hand-colored etching</u> and a poster. That's why it's far more likely for a rare print to "slip through the cracks" than an <u>original</u> painting by a widely-recognized master.

As with one-of-a-kind works, proper identification of a printed piece's media and value characteristics is key to turning a profit as a picker. Let's examine the most frequent print types you'll be confronted with as a picker, how to identify them, and where they place within the Value Pyramid:

1. Engravings/Woodblocks/Linocuts

As with the media for one-of-a-kind artworks, the printmaking techniques that top the value pyramid are, for the most part, older, more established techniques that historical artists used and approved of. Rembrandt is famous for his <u>etchings</u>; <u>woodblocks</u> were the preferred printmaking technique for Masters from the Far East; and while <u>linocuts</u> didn't come about until the 20th century, the technique was utilized by heavyweights like Henri Matisse, M. C. Escher and Pablo Picasso.

These techniques require extensive involvement from the artist from start to finish. Although the processes differ, for each one the artist must design, sketch, etch and cut to create the <u>composition</u> within the source material (metal, wood and linoleum, respectively), then actively "pull" the print from its source <u>plate</u> or <u>block</u> after it has been inked and put through a press.

They are also intrinsically limited by their nature. The copper plate used in traditional <u>etchings</u> and <u>engravings</u>, for example, will wear-out after about 300 pressings, and the first <u>prints</u> (or "impressions") will be of far superior quality to the 300th. The only thing that limits more modern printing techniques are the arbitrary numbers assigned to them as part of a self-imposed "<u>limited edition</u>," and the last copy will look exactly the same as the first. (For that reason, when it comes to modern printing techniques like <u>offset lithography</u>, an early print should have the same monetary value as one later in the edition.)

Etchings and Engravings fall into the "<u>Intaglio</u>" family of printing, which also includes variations such as <u>Aquatint</u>, <u>Mezzotint</u> and <u>Drypoint</u>. The differences between these processes and their visual effects range from subtle to significant, but the process of identification is similar and value disparity is minimal. The easiest way to identify Intaglio prints is by their plate marks. A plate mark is the impression that a metal printing plate leaves in the paper when it has been pressed. It will

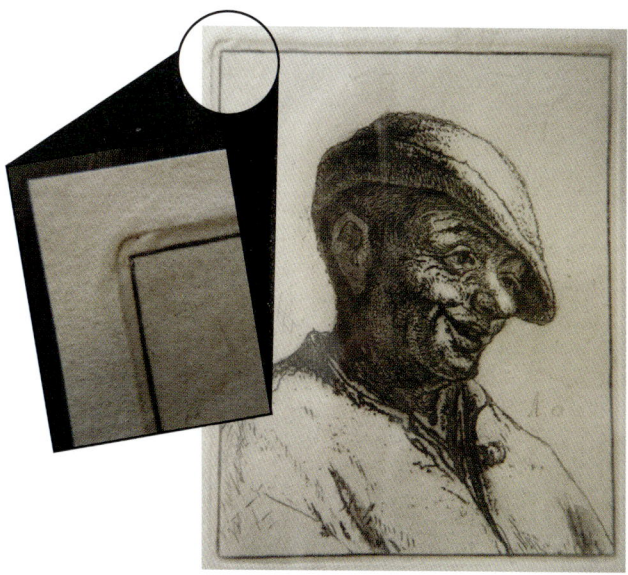

Close-up of the Plate Mark on Adriaen Van Ostade's "Laughing Peasant" (17th Century). These impressions in the paper are the most identifiable characteristic of etchings and engravings.

Please Note:

Some famous artists, like Rembrandt, did their own etching and engraving; however, reproductions of many artists' works were done by independent engravers. (In the days before photography and mass-tourism, that was the only way many people could ever hope to see famous museum pieces.) In these cases, there will typically be some sort of inscription in the print's margin that references both the original artist and the engraver. As you might expect, etchings and engravings done by the original artist generally have more value.

look like an embossed border around the image—from a few millimeters to several inches outside the composition—with rounded corners (sharp corners on the printing plate would damage the paper).

Woodcuts and linocuts are forms of "relief" printing created using a chisel or gouge to cut a relief image into the plank side of a block of wood in the case of woodcuts, or linoleum in the case of linocuts. These prints typically exhibit a lack of fine detail and have a carved appearance when viewed. They are often "black and white" (or whatever color ink was used, plus the paper color), but can be rendered in color if a separate block or linoleum sheet is carved for each color. As with stone lithography and serigraphs, other media for which each color must be laid individually, the colors will generally be uniform in application and consistent in tone.

2. Stone Lithographs/Photogravure/Serigraphs

These methods of reproduction are more practical for large scale production. They were initially utilized for commercial purposes, before being adapted and adopted by fine artists as a viable means to reproduce their work.

When stone lithography became popular in the early 19th century, it was the first major printmaking technique to emerge in 300 years. Although it was originally invented by a German actor as a cheap means to reproduce theatrical works, it became popular with artists because it allowed them to print art organically. Rather than etching or carving an image, the artist could naturally "paint" or "draw" it on a flat stone (traditionally limestone). Unfortunately, complex compositions that utilized many colors required the creation of multiple stones, sometimes weighing three-hundred pounds apiece, which quickly ratcheted up time and expense (not to mention back problems). The stone lithography used in cigar box labels, for example, involved as many as twenty stones and cost up to $6,000 to produce—big money in the 19th century. As is the case with most print media, stone lithography lost popularity as cheaper and easier methods of reproduction became available during the 20th century.

Stone lithographs are identifiable by their relatively small number of richly consistent colors. There will be no surface texture (unless the paper is embossed, or hand-embellishments were added post-production) and, upon close inspection, you'll probably notice a speckling effect in the paper. This is due to the surface texture of the limestone printing surface. Additionally, you may see a stippling pattern within the composition. As stone lithography evolved, artists began stippling individual stones with a network of dots that would, when placed against the other colors, create variant degrees of shading. While modern offset lithography features a network of mechanically-created dots, the stippling in stone lithography is hand-applied to the stone, and thus will feature variations in pattern, application and size.

Photogravure, as you might guess from the name, combines photography and engraving. The process developed along with photography during the 19th Century, and entailed creating photographic images on copper plates that could then be etched. The technique was originally used purely as a photographic process, as it reproduced the detail and tones in a black-and-white photograph quite nicely; however, it was eventually adapted as a means of reproducing fine art prints

and paintings. As Photogravure is a form of Intaglio printing, the process of identification is the same as with etchings
and <u>engravings</u> (i.e., look for the <u>plate marks</u>). However, as the
process involves photography—a mechanical means of <u>repro-
duction</u> frowned upon by some purists—it typically will not
carry the same values (all things being equal). Photogravure
reproductions of paintings and prints will also typically carry
some sort of inscription (usually printed beneath the image)
that refers to the original work and artist.

Andy Warhol single-handedly changed people's perception of screen printing, which until the 1960s was considered
a cheap-and-easy way to produce T-shirts and advertising
posters. His use of an intentionally commercial media with intentionally non-aesthetic subjects, like Campbell's Soup cans,
turned the art world on its ear and helped turn unglamorous
screen printing into glamorous fine art "serigraphs."

Serigraphs are produced by creating a stencil on a thin fab-
ric like silk. These "silk screens," one for each color, are then
placed on paper or canvas and a squeegee with ink is pulled
across it, leaving ink on the paper where the stencil is open.
Like linocuts and stone lithography, other media in which
each color is laid separately, the colors will be uniform and
consistent in tone. However, the inks used in serigraphs are
opaque and will give the print a subtle surface texture. As a result, serigraphs appear more "painterly" than most other prints.

3. Offset Lithography and Digital Prints (Giclees)

These are modern and mechanical methods used for printing in mass quantities. Because these processes involve printers, computers and photography—often at the expense of the

This serigraph by Jim Buckels showcases the solid blocks of colors, individually applied through a stencil, quintessential of the media. The blow-up better shows the media's texture and layered effect.

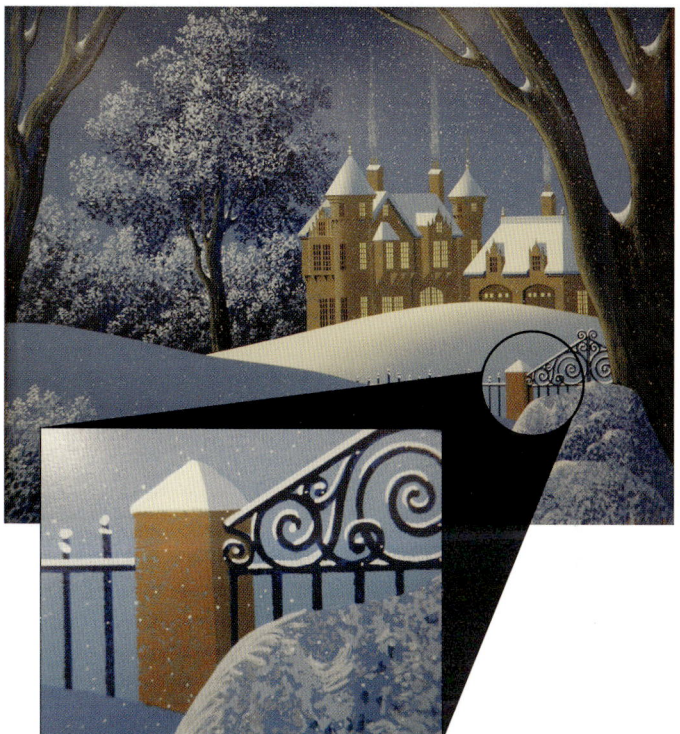

artist's own involvement in the process—they are generally considered less collectible than other graphic media.

Offset lithography is the most common method of commercial printing, and is used in the production of newspapers, magazines and posters. In offset lithography, art and text is placed on thin metal <u>plates</u> which are dampened with water and ink by rollers on the press. The oil-based ink adheres to the image area, while the water clings to the non-image area. The inked area is then transferred (or "offset") to a rubber cylinder and then onto the paper as it passes around it. This is sometimes referred to as "four color" printing as only four colors are used: cyan, magenta, yellow and black. These variations of the primary colors (blue, red and yellow), plus black, are used to create every other color in the spectrum. However, rather than mixing the colors the way an artist would on a palate, each color is applied individually in a tiny network of dots that, when arranged next to the other dot colors, causes our brain to combine them in a way that produces every color of the rainbow. Cool, huh?

These dots are also the key to identifying <u>offset lithographic prints</u>, because although they are too small for our eyes and brain to process individually, they are easily detectable by a magnifying glass with at least 5X magnification. Under magnification, they will appear uniform and grid-like, almost like a honeycomb. Be sure to check the signature, too. If it has the

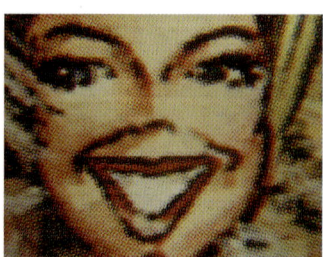 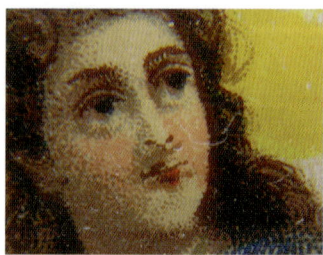

Under magnification, the image on the left shows the mechanically produced dots of a modern offset lithograph, while the image on the right shows the hand-applied stippling of a 19th century stone lithograph.

same pattern, then the signature is part of the print (or "plate-signed" as people in the art world often call it). If it doesn't, then there's a good chance that the artist added their own hand-signature to the lithograph. (In this case there will often be two signatures: a "plate signature" from the printed image, and a secondary hand-signature added by the artist sometime after the print's production.)

Offset lithographs may be bonded to canvas and other materials (like Masonite board). This process is called "transferring" and, by adhering the paper prints to a more artistic support, gives them a look closer to that of an original. Fortunately, the dots will still be visible under magnification, so as long as you have your trusty magnifying glass handy, you won't be fooled.

Digital prints and "Giclees" (a French term meaning "to squirt") are essentially ink jet prints on paper and canvas. They're difficult to rank, because their quality ranges from poor to excellent and the term has been assigned to everything from high-end publishing houses utilizing state-of-the-art Iris printers to art fair artists running them off an Epson in their basement. For the purpose of this book, however, I have them ranked at the bottom of the pyramid. First of all, they've only been around for twenty years so you're not likely to encounter them in many of your prime picking places. Secondly, the resale market for contemporary living artists is spotty at best, and

Please Note:
As "Giclees" can be produced directly onto canvas, they are often "embellished" (see page 57) which will result in surface texture at specific areas of the print.

not an area you want to be concentrating your efforts anyway. Thirdly, the permanence of the media is still in question, as even some giclees from prominent publishers and artists have begun to crack and fade in a very short period of time.

Large Iris printers have the ability to print directly onto canvas and high-quality papers. These inks absorb naturally into the <u>support</u>, and as the colors are "mixed" rather than individually applied, produce most of the subtle color transitions and shading you'll see in an original artwork. The inks provide no surface texture; however, and sharp borders will typically delineate the edge of the printed part of the image.

As with original artworks, the list of printing techniques appearing in the Value Pyramid is not comprehensive; however, I've tried to represent the vast majority of printed artworks you'll come across. Whenever possible, try to be mindful of the periods in which an artist worked and what media was accessible to them at the time. I once had a client rush excitedly into my office saying that they had just purchased an original Picasso giclee. Needless to say, they didn't leave my office quite as excited.

Now you have a general understanding of fine art and fine art printing techniques, how to identify them, and where they rank, value wise, in the wonderful world of art collecting. Certainly there are exceptions to every rule. For example, Andy Warhol's serigraphs, an artistic process for which he was a pioneer, can sell for millions while his original sketches can often be had for a few thousand. However, the Value Pyramid should provide a framework for which to rank and assess your discoveries.

A Few Words About Sculpture

I haven't spent a lot of time discussing <u>sculpture</u>, nor have I ranked it within the <u>Value Pyramid</u>. That's primarily because it's an extremely challenging media to inspect and critique in the field, and without specific connoisseurship, can be a guessing game. The materials, treatment and presentation of art on canvas and paper have evolved significantly over the last 500 years, while <u>sculpture</u>—from bronze "<u>lost wax</u>" castings to hand-chiseled marble—has remained virtually unchanged for THOUSANDS of years. Just like with a woman, be careful making assumptions about a sculpture's age based on its appearance. The finish, or <u>patina</u>, on bronze changes over time, but contemporary sculptures are often given decorative patinas to appear old, while antique sculptures can be treated to look just like new. Stone sculpture may not age at all.

The good news is, unlike works on <u>canvas</u> and paper, there is usually an intrinsic value to sculpted material. Purchase an <u>etching</u> in poor condition by a bad artist, and you've basically paid to haul off someone else's garbage. Purchase a bronze sculpture by a bad artist, and it will still have scrap value. As of the publishing of this book, brass and bronze have a scrap value of about $3/lb. That means if you purchase a fifty pound bronze of a weasel for $50, you should be able to scrap it for about $150. Woo Hoo!

However, unless you have a truck, a strong back, and a buddy at a local <u>foundry</u>, buying sculpture just to scrap it is no path to riches. As with other media, the first step to picking sculpture successfully is attributing the work to a specific artist. Most fine art sculptures will feature an artist's signature somewhere—usually engraved around its base. Sometimes, a signature will be accompanied with, or replaced by, a foundry mark—a monogram, initial, or other design indicating where the work was cast. This can provide important clues to the work's provenance. In the absence of a signature or foundry mark, a purchase should only be made if you feel confident the work will sell based on its decorative quality. Otherwise, be sure to have Mr. Smelter on speed dial.

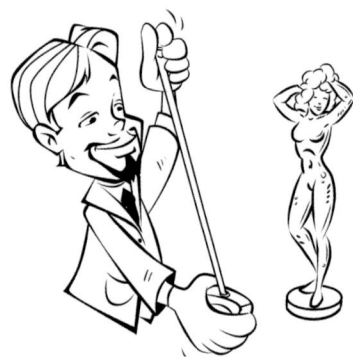

Brett Says: "**Be aware, sculptors usually don't have ease of picking in mind when they sign. It's not uncommon for a signature to be placed beneath a block of hand-carved alabaster or on the inner-thigh of a cow within a bronze stampede.**"

One last warning—sculptures are frequently "recast" from existing sculptures, especially if the artist is deceased and copyrights have either expired or were never instituted. Sculpted bronzes by Frederic Remington, for example, have been recast so much through the years that they've lost much of their detail and collectible value. (You can find recasts for sale online for a few hundred dollars.) Still, if you can confidently attribute a sculpture to a noted artist, and it can be had for a good price, it is worth considering.

Nit-Picking and Cherry-Picking
(Other Characteristics Influencing Value)

Now that you've studied the Value Pyramid, and are familiar with the types of art you'll be presented with as a picker, it's time to explore additional characteristics that will influence an artwork's value (positively and negatively). Knowing these characteristics is crucial to becoming a successful picker. Remember, for the purposes of this book, being a "successful picker" is all about turning your discoveries into cash. As a result, some of my advice may seem counterintuitive at first blush. For example, consider the following scenario:

Picker A finds a 17th century Italian school <u>etching</u> of a mother and child. It's in decent shape, has clear <u>plate marks</u>, and its <u>composition</u> is intact. He buys it for $20.

Picker B is directed to a musty old <u>oil</u> painting signed by "Van-something" by the proprietor of a local antique mall. His heart races as he sees that the work, a still-life of poppies in a vase, is actually signed "Van Gogh." He buys it for $100.

Which was the better pick? If you go strictly by my Value Pyramid the answer may seem obvious, but what if I told you Picker A was able to sell his etching to a dealer for $100 later that afternoon, while Picker B spent several years and thousands of dollars trying to get his Van Gogh authenticated, and was still trying? Seem farfetched? My company once worked with a client who spent six-figures getting a prospective Vincent Van Gogh painting authenticated—and still hadn't obtained enough authenticity to it sell it through proper channels.

While no experts would denounce it as inauthentic, none were willing to risk proclaiming it as authentic either.

Provenance

The more you know about a particular piece of artwork, the better. As our friend Teri Horton discovered, a lack of <u>provenance</u> (history) on an artwork means more time, expense, and no guarantee of a satisfactory resolution.

Documentation of an artwork's provenance can be written or verbal. Written is better, of course, as memories are foggy and often embellished, but even vague verbal testimony can provide clues (i.e., "my Grandfather brought this back from Germany during the war"). Other examples of provenance you may find with an artwork include its date of completion, title, artist's biography, and <u>certificate of authenticity</u>. Be sure to check behind the work, as sometimes this information is written on the back of a <u>canvas</u> or affixed to its verso. Even a sticker from a long-departed <u>gallery</u> or frame shop can provide important clues about time-period and location.

> **Please Note:**
> Inaccurate or fabricated provenance is worse than no provenance at all. I can't tell you how many times I've heard, "but it had a Certificate!" from clients disappointed with my assessment of their artworks. Paperwork on an artwork is only as viable as the person or entity behind it. Do your homework, and if important documentation is boilerplate and signed illegibly by no one in particular, run away.

Artist Signature

The artist's signature is a basic form of written <u>provenance</u>, and probably the absolute minimum you'll want as a picker. As an appraiser, unsigned works are the bane of my existence. It is extremely difficult to attribute an unsigned painting with no provenance to a specific artistic period or movement, much less a specific artist. If you do purchase an unsigned artwork, be prepared for the additional expense of having an expert look at it, or be prepared to re-sell it based solely on its decorative/antiquity value.

There are many reasons a painting could be unsigned: It could be a replication of a masterwork, which will often be unsigned in deference to the original artist; it could be from a "school" of art, such as the <u>Hudson River School</u>, where plein air paintings were often left unattributed; or it could be by an amateur artist unhappy with the work. Keep in mind, some artists sign the verso of the canvas so as to not obscure their <u>compositions</u>, while others intentionally hid their signatures. (18th Century Spanish Master, Francisco de Goya, was famous for this.) Also, signatures on older works can sometimes be obscured by dirt. Check carefully!

Illegible signatures aren't much better. (How an artist could think that signing like a drunken doctor writing a prescription would help their legacy is beyond me. Is it coincidence that the vast majority of artists who have stood the test of time have signatures that are both distinctive *and* legible? I think not.) Still, a few discernible letters and an alphabetical listing of important artists, like <u>The Artist's Bluebook</u>, may provide you—or an expert you consult with—enough clues for identification.

Just to make things a tad more confusing, some famous artists, like Toulouse Lautrec, Thomas Moran and Albrecht Durer, preferred stylish monograms over traditional signatures. These monograms are actually pretty easy to identify once you're familiar with them, but becoming familiar with them takes time. (See pages 77-79 for some helpful resources.)

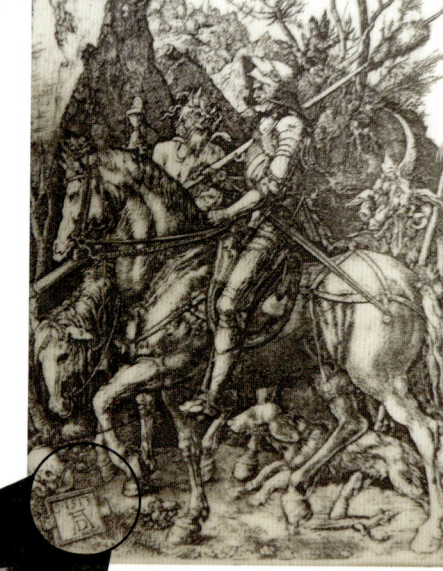

Blow-up of Albrecht Durer's monogram as it appears on his engraving, "Knight, Death and the Devil."

When it comes to prints, most are "<u>plate-signed</u>," which means the artist's signature is physically part of the <u>reproduction</u>. These plate signatures typically appear within the <u>composition</u> in the same location the signature appeared on the <u>original</u> work. If the work has a second signature, usually within the print's margin, then there's a good chance it was added by the artist. This will add additional value. A magnifying glass can often help detect if a work is plate-signed, hand-signed, or both.

Condition

As a picker, you're not going to find many artworks in "<u>mint condition</u>." If a painting has been left on the floor of a cluttered storage unit, it probably hasn't been taken great care of. Since condition is of paramount importance to value, that's a major concern.

Not all damage is created equal, however. Some flaws are negligible in their impact to value, while others are catastrophic. As you might expect, the more damage impacts the integrity of a <u>composition</u> and adversely affects its overall aesthetic, the more it will negatively impact its value potential. For example, if a print has minor acid damage within its margin, then it may be worth taking a chance on. However, if the image itself is torn, discolored, and stained, you're probably better off passing.

Most damage can be repaired by a competent conservator. I've seen <u>conservators</u> perform miracles on artworks I suspected were done for. However, as with most of this book, it's all about determining the feasibility and cost effectiveness of doing so. Would you pay a conservator $1,000 to restore a flood-damaged <u>lithograph</u> worth $5? Of course not.

Works on <u>canvas</u> are more forgiving—both in terms of the impact damage has on their overall value, and the impact of their repair on your wallet. Some damage, such as <u>craquelure</u> (the fine network of cracking you'll sometimes see in antique paintings), can be a natural effect of <u>aging</u> and, as long as it doesn't noticeably detract from the <u>composition</u>, will not significantly impact its value. Other blemishes can often be repaired by a competent frame shop, rather than a specialized (and much more expensive) art conservator. For example, dimpling and creasing in a <u>canvas</u> can often be reduced or eliminated through steaming and/or re-stretching. Many frame shops also offer canvas cleaning services, which can remove surface stains and brighten colors that have grown dingy through an accumulation of dirt, dust, and airborne carcinogens. Better yet, these services are relatively cheap and can aid in a painting's resale. (You'd spend $10 to wash a car you're trying to sell, right?) More serious repairs, such as punctures in the canvas or paint loss, should be left to a professional restorer and, at that point, you'll want to weigh the cost effectiveness of doing so. Keep in mind, however, that patching or relining (supporting a thinning canvas from behind with a second canvas), may be less expensive than you might think.

Paint loss is the biggest bugaboo. Once paint begins to flake off a canvas, only significant and time-consuming repairs can restore a painting's integrity and aesthetic. This type of <u>restoration</u> is expensive, and even if the composition is restored to "like new" from an appearance standpoint, the overall value of the artwork will still take a hit. Why? Whenever someone other than the original artist adds brushstrokes to a canvas, it adversely impacts its perceived purity among fine art collectors. Of course, if the restoration is done by a recognized and competent fine art conservator, then the value gained by restoring the work will far outweigh the value loss inherent in its having been restored; however, if the work is repaired/restored improperly (i.e., noticeable color variation, added <u>compositional</u> elements, significant <u>overpainting</u> of the artist's original work, etc.) then the loss of value could be catastrophic.

Brett Says: "**If your'e curious whether your pick may have been restored, head to the closet with a blacklight.**
Resorations typically show up as dark purple areas under ultraviolet light!"

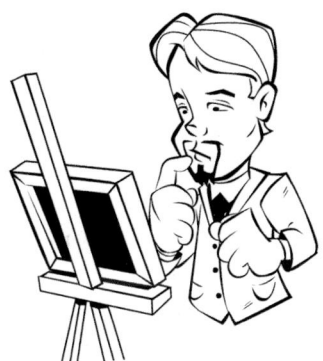

Works on paper are more susceptible to damage and their values are more dramatically impacted by it. Think of <u>prints</u> like baseball cards. A Mickey Mantle rookie card in good condition may be worth thousands, but that same card, placed in the spokes of a bicycle and autographed by your cousin Buck, is probably worthless.

To make matters worse, evaluating the condition of

framed prints in the field is a little like guessing which present to open first on Christmas morning. You can pick it up, check the tag, and admire the packaging … but there's still a chance you'll be disappointed when you unwrap it. The portion of the art visible within the frame may look great, but its presentation (frame, glass, matting, backing board, etc.) could hide mold, mildew, <u>acid burns</u> … or worse. A client once brought me a vintage poster that had been hanging on the wall of his home. It looked in decent shape, but under a magnifying glass I noticed critters scurrying under the glass. Turns out, termites had burrowed through the client's wall, and into the artwork from behind. They then proceeded to nest while feasting on the wood pulp in the paper and its backing board. Yuck!

To help minimize the chance you get stuck with a lump of coal in your Christmas stocking, here are a few flaws you'll frequently find festering in frames:

1. *Fading*: is irreversible and can be crippling to a <u>print's</u> value. Subtle fading may not be noticeable unless inspected alongside an unfaded example of the same print, or when removed from the frame. (Sometimes a print's matting will cover the edge of the <u>composition</u> and reveal a clear delineation in color.) However, if you notice a "bluish" tinge to a print that you suspect was once vibrant (blues fade slower than other colors), then you should probably pass.

2. *Foxing* (right): These are small reddish-brown stains that typically look like a network of stars on paper prints. These are caused by fungal activity, or a chemical breakdown of the paper resulting from non-<u>conservational</u> materials. These are usually repairable, but are ugly and adversely affect an artwork's aesthetic. A few here and there are probably not deal breakers, but if that "network of stars" looks more like a galaxy, then run far, far away.

3. *Moisture*: <u>Foxing</u> can sometimes be a symptom of an even greater problem—moisture. Get an antique print wet within non-conservational framing and you'll have a veritable Petri dish in a few years. Check the work's matting and backing. If there are signs of <u>buckling</u> within the matting, or moisture staining on the <u>print's</u> dust cover or backing board, you'll want to pass (and wash your hands). Keep in mind that water-based media, like <u>watercolor</u>, will often cause a natural buckling or waviness in the paper <u>support</u>. That is of no concern.

4. *Yellowing*: This can result from UV (ultraviolet) light exposure, non-conservational framing materials, or a breakdown of the paper. If the yellowing is mild and uniform, then the impact to value may be minimal, but if it's splotchy and adversely impacts the overall aesthetic of the piece, then it will probably need to be restored.

5. *Acid-Burn* (right): These are specific areas of discoloration resulting from non-conservational "<u>acidic</u>" framing materials making contact with the work's surface or support. This can be due to the work's window matting (which produces a halo-effect around the piece called "Mat

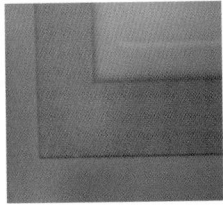

Burn") or the use of <u>acidic</u> backing materials like newsprint or corrugated cardboard. Some antique prints were even backed with plywood slats that, over time, would transfer their wood-grain directly to the print itself, knotholes and all! (If you can determine the age of a tree by counting the rings in your print, that's a bad sign.)

Please Note:
You can often tell if matting is <u>acidic</u> by the inner edge that borders the art (called a "bevel"). If its color is dingy and looks coffee-stained, then it's probably acidic.

Most of the flaws mentioned above will weaken the structural integrity of a work on paper over time—eventually causing it to become brittle and crumble away. That's why condition is of paramount importance to value and why you should immediately work to preserve your paper picks (see page 74).

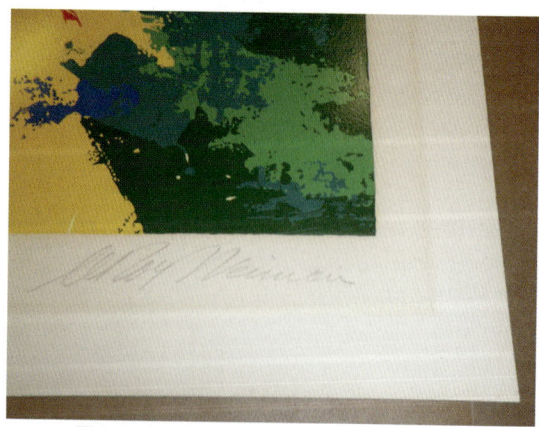

This LeRoy Neiman serigraph exhibits both yellowing and acid-burn

Limited Edition

Typically this entails the numbering of a print as part of a series of identical images. This series could be as few as one (a <u>monoprint</u>), or more than 100,000. (Not exactly "limited," is it?)

As we've discussed, most early <u>printing</u> techniques were limited by their nature. It wasn't until well into the 20th century, when prints became big business and techniques allowed for nearly infinite numbers of reproductions, that <u>limited editions</u> (also called "<u>signed and numbered prints</u>") became popular. A limited edition <u>print</u> is typically numbered in pencil within the print's left margin, and signed by the artist in the lower-right. Usually there are two numbers separated by a forward slash—the number on the left denotes the number of the print, while the number on the right denotes the size of the entire edition.

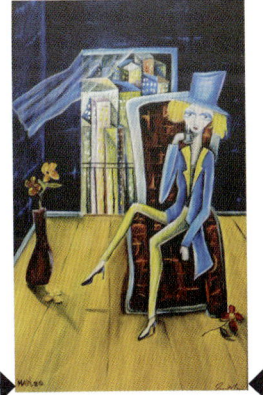

"Coffee Break," a limited edition Giclee by Jennifer Main, has a printed "plate" signature in the lower-left, along with its year of completion and a "circle c" copyright symbol. In the lower-right, the work has been hand-signed and numbered 21 out of an edition of 325.

Since rarity is an important value characteristic in art, it probably won't surprise you when I say that the smaller the edition, the better. <u>Limited edition</u> prints went a little crazy in the 1980s and 1990s, and the <u>edition sizes</u> for <u>prints</u> by popular artists like Beverly Doolittle and Thomas Kinkade grew astronomical. Fortunately, the trend has recently gone back towards more exclusive editions. Keep in mind, some artists get around this exclusivity by issuing multiple editions of the same piece in different sizes, or as individual editions of "<u>Proof Prints</u>."

Proof Prints

<u>Proof Prints</u> are usually identified with initials within a print's margin, and typically represent a small number of prints published apart from a larger edition of the same image. The most common designations are as follows: <u>Artist's Proof</u> (A.P.), <u>Publisher Proof</u> (P.P.), <u>Hors de Commerce Proofs</u> (H.C.) and <u>Épreuve d'artiste</u> (E.A.).

Back in the early-to-mid 20th century, the early days of <u>limited edition</u> printing, Proof Prints were a crucial step in the

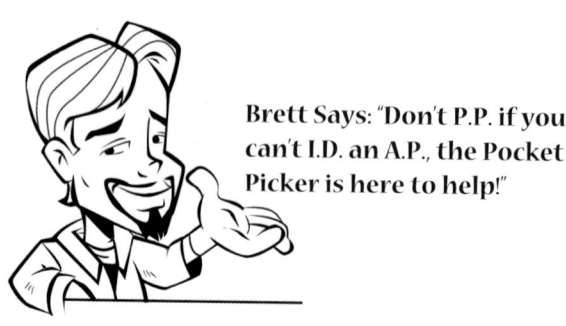

Brett Says: "Don't P.P. if you can't I.D. an A.P., the Pocket Picker is here to help!"

publishing process. The first few prints were physically inspected by the artist or publisher in order to confirm such things as color correctness, integrity of the image, etc., and were designated as such so that the printers could use them as a quality benchmark for subsequent prints in the edition. These Proof Prints became desirable by collectors because, ostensibly, the artist was more involved in the process.

Proof Prints became so popular and demanded by collectors that, eventually, the designations lost most of their practical meaning and became simply another way to squeeze a few more prints into an edition at a higher price. Even worse, it was easy for a disreputable dealer, gallery, or print owner with a number 2 pencil, to designate a signed, open edition print as an "A.P." and resell it at a much higher price.

As a result, much of the luster, and added value, has vanished from prints designated as Proofs. Assuming authenticity, a legitimate Proof Print may still have additional value because of its exclusivity in relation to the larger, signed and numbered edition. However, as a picker you should be leery of unnumbered Proof Prints, especially those by prominent (and frequently forged) 20th century graphic artists like Picasso, Dali, Miro and Chagall. In most cases, it's safer to pick from the main "signed and numbered edition" as the quantity is known and the numbering makes it easier to account for and authenticate.

Remarques

A remarque is a small, original sketch which typically appears in a print's margin or on its verso. Sometimes, remarques are planned additions to a special edition of prints and applied before their release, or they could be added by the artist at a later date. (Artists appearing at art shows or openings will often add <u>remarques</u> or other personalizations to a client's purchase.) Depending on its size, detail and <u>medium</u>, the value a remarque adds to a print could be greater than the print itself. For

Please Note:
Check the remarque under magnification. Occasionally, remarques appearing within a print's margin are part of the reproduction and not original.

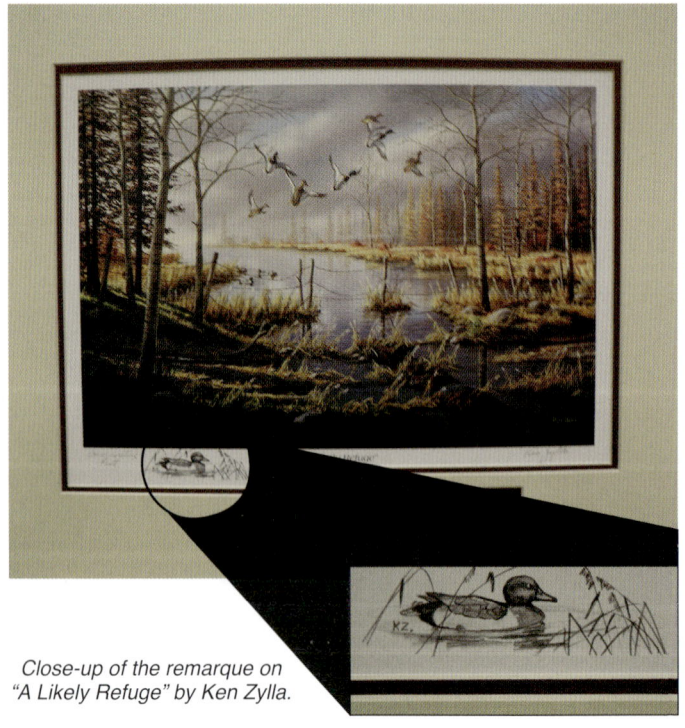

Close-up of the remarque on "A Likely Refuge" by Ken Zylla.

example, if small pencil <u>sketches</u> by an artist routinely sell for $500, you can expect a comparably-sized remarque in pencil to enhance the value of a $20 poster by roughly the same amount.

Embellishments

<u>Embellishments</u> are additional brushstrokes added to a printed piece. Artists have been hand-coloring etchings for centuries, while more contemporary artists have begun adding acrylic embellishments to giclees.

Embellishments, as long as they are added by the <u>original</u> artist, will almost always add value. Be aware, however, that embellishments are sometimes added by the publisher or another artisan. (Currier and Ives <u>prints</u>—timeless views of log cabins, horse-drawn carriages, and other iconic images of 19th Century Americana—were, ironically, embellished by an assembly line of immigrant German women.) As long as the embellishments were endorsed and authorized by the original artist(s), then they will still, in all likelihood, add value; however, a few dabs of clear <u>acrylic</u> dolloped on a reprinted Van Gogh by a contemporary publisher will offer no value beyond aesthetic.

Framing

From a Picker's perspective, framing is usually an unwanted obstacle. It can hide conditional flaws, poor framing technique (such as taping or gluing), <u>provenance</u> (such as copyright dates and publishing information), and even artist signatures and inscriptions. For that reason, most collectors of vintage prints prefer them to be unframed.

On top of that, they're cumbersome and rarely have much resale value on their own. We've all heard the expression "The frame is worth more than the picture," and I can't deny that hand-carved gilt frames can be valuable (sometimes thousands of dollars), but you're far more likely to find decorative frames made to look opulent through plaster cast embellishments and gold paint. That said, if you suspect a frame to be antique and hand-crafted, take it to a reputable framer for inspection.

Picking My Brain
(Picking Tips and Strategies)

I could end this book right now, and you'd have most of the information you'd need to make solid picks in the field. Of course, experience is the best teacher, and the more you analyze artwork the better at it you'll become. With practice, you'll be able to identify facsimile signatures without a magnifying glass, smell the difference between oil and acrylic paints, and determine the age of a painting by the type of <u>canvas</u>!

You'll also begin to develop certain "Picking Precepts"—general rules about the picking of fine art that will assist you in the process of picking profitably. For example, you may discover that Western art sells like hotcakes in your area, or make a contact that collects antique Japanese <u>woodblocks</u>, or discover a hot young local artist who is rapidly on the rise. These are facts that will influence how and what you pick.

Until you're able to develop your own Picking Precepts, you can borrow a few of mine. Over the last twenty years, I've worked as an appraiser, an art dealer, a retail gallery Director, and a picker/collector. As a result, I've seen the market from all sides and have a pretty good idea of what sells, how much it should sell for, and why. Combine these general rules with the ones you develop from your own experiences, and you'll soon become a force in the picking world.

Old Does Not Equal Valuable

This is the most common misconception of amateur pickers. There were plenty of bad artists in the 18th Century just like there are bad artists today. Some people get a kick out of collecting antique artworks, but a bad painting by an unknown artist isn't going to appeal to a connoisseur regardless of when it was rendered.

Of course, recognizing "bad" art isn't always easy. Beauty is in the eye of the beholder, as the cliché goes; however, if the work is badly composed, has poor <u>perspective</u>, and depicts subject matter few people would hang in their home, then you should probably pass.

Avoid Portraiture

Speaking of art most people won't hang in their homes. If you know the artist is of significant esteem or if the portrait is the spitting image of a famous and collectible International icon (like Marilyn Monroe, for example) then feel free to snatch it up, but if it's an unknown portrait by an unknown artist, then leave it for some unknown buyer.

Before photography, painted <u>portraiture</u> was the only way to commemorate loved ones. Most artists, from Da Vinci down, dabbled in it, but unlike Leonardo's world famous depiction of "Mona" Lisa del Giocondo, most portraiture is only of interest to the people who commissioned it. Most people would just as soon hang an 8" by 10" photo of your Uncle Charlie in their home as a portrait of some 17th century silk merchant.

Eschew the Ordinary

Many people, myself included, grew up watching Bob Ross' "Joy of Painting" during the 1980s and 1990s. Each week, Mr. Ross would compose a <u>landscape</u> of snow-covered mountains and tree-lined lakes. The scenes were well-composed and rendered … but monotonous. They could've been set anywhere—the Rocky Mountains, the Swiss Alps, you name it—and as a result lack distinctiveness.

With all due respect to Mr. Ross, who painted the scenes as a teaching tool, these are artworks to avoid. They're an indication of an emerging artist honing their skill, or a painting intended for decorative purposes. Sears sold a series of these types of artworks—lonely cabins at the base of snow-capped

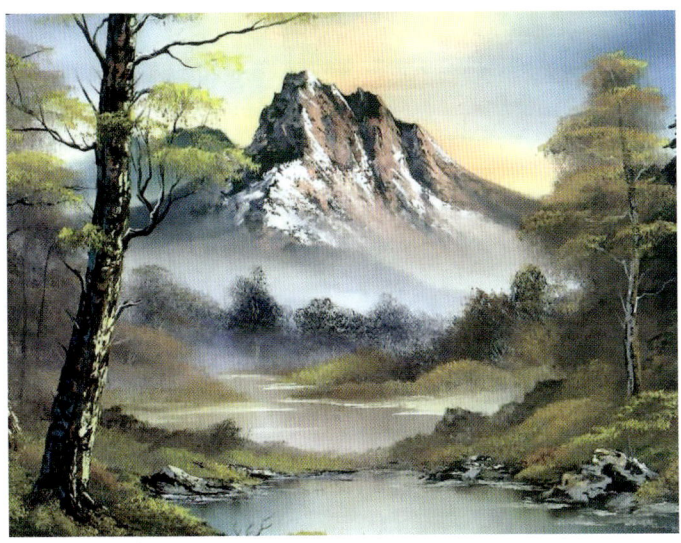

This landscape painting may look pretty … but it's about as generic as you get.

hills—during the 1960s and '70s to complement their home furnishings. Other home décor companies followed suit, and soon walls were full of generic artworks, painted by generic studio artists, and signed with generic surnames like "Smith." Most of these artworks are currently for sale on eBay. In recent years, China has taken over this practice (surprise, surprise). Their assembly line creations can be found at fine supermarkets everywhere.

Conversely, the more original a work is, the less likely it was done as decorative wall-filler by a studio or emerging artist. Few artists render Cubist cityscapes, while virtually every artist, at one time or another, has painted a realistic floral still-life. That's not to say the still-life couldn't have value—and it may be easier to sell for its decorative value (there's a reason so many artists paint them)—but with few exceptions, the artists that have stood the test of time have forged their own unique artistic identity.

Be Leery of "Art 101" Artists

These are the artists nearly everyone has heard of. We've all heard a story about the _____ (insert "Art 101" artist's name: Pablo Picasso, Pierre-Auguste Renoir, Marc Chagall, Salvador Dali, etc.) that was purchased at a garage sale for $5. It has been known to happen, as it did with an original Andy Warhol sketch I appraised a couple years ago (more on the extenuating circumstances associated with that in a bit), but big scores like that are the exception rather than the rule. Don't expect them.

"Huh?" I hear you saying. "Why would I avoid an artwork by a master?" You wouldn't, of course, but if living in Vegas for over twenty years has taught me anything, it's that you have to play the odds. Investing in blue-chip artists is a viable strategy if you're a millionaire buying esteemed artworks through respected dealers or auction houses, but expecting to profit picking pawned Picasso paintings in Portland? Phooey!

Works by Masters are frequently reproduced and replicated—they're also frequently forged. This is especially true with 20th century masters like Picasso, Dali and Chagall—three artists who were ridiculously prolific and popular during their lifetime, and whose vigorous use of modern printing processes made the path to impropriety even easier. Criminals, like most people, take the path of least resistance, and it's far easier and more profitable to fudge Picasso's signature on an unsigned lithograph than recreate an oil painting by a mid-tier artist like Johann Berthelsen.

Focus on Middle Tier Artists

Since you don't want to purchase bad art from no-name artists (unless you need inventory for your own garage sale), and you don't want to spend significant time and money pursuing authenticity for that "Picasso" painting that miraculously found its way into a Goodwill auction, middle tier artists should be your primary focus. A mid-tier artist offers an active collector base and secondary market, but isn't so famous that it's impossible to believe their work could have slipped through the cracks (and its value won't be as negatively affected for having done so). Additionally, should it be necessary, works by middle tier artists are far easier to appraise and authenticate. The pool of recognized experts for Masters is small, their fees are large, and their results are never guaranteed.

Right now, you're probably saying, "that sounds great, Brett, but what's the 'middle tier' and how do I recognize an artist who's in it?" I define a mid-tier artist as one who is "listed" (an artist who has gained recognition through awards and prestigious gallery and/or museum exhibitions) and whose works sell at values beyond decorative. Your Aunt Tilly may be a heck of a painter, and she may sell her florals at the local art fair for a hundred dollars each, but nobody buys them as an investment, or because "Tilly the Great" painted them. They buy them because they're pretty and look great over the commode.

However, let's say Aunt Tilly wins an art show, gets featured at a prestigious museum, and Bill Gates purchases one of her works. Suddenly, Aunt Tilly is hobnobbing with jetsetters who purchase her art from galleries along Madison Avenue, while your letters go unanswered. Aunt Tilly has graduated from the "lower tier," where most "starving" and emerging artists reside, to the "middle tier" of collectible listed artists.

Fortunately for today's picker, identifying the Aunt Tilly's of the art world has never been easier. There are numerous online and published resources (see pages 77-79) that document listed artists. Many times, a simple Internet search will give you an indication of just how well-known a particular artist is. Finding an artist's name in "Google" is no guarantee their work is collectible, but not finding it virtually assures that it isn't.

Pick Artists with "Staying Power"

By "staying power" I mean the artist's long-term value potential. Animated olives high-diving into martini glasses may be cute and conversational over the bar in your den, but what will that artwork fetch on the secondary market twenty years from now? History is littered with flash-in-the-pan artists that rode the coattails of other artists, or capitalized on a kitschy trend that died-away over time. This isn't a huge concern for pickers, as the market (or lack thereof) for most of the artists you'll be picking from will be fairly established, and if you're turning pieces quickly, then trends and fads won't affect you as much. However, if an artwork appears "dated" then that will negatively impact its market, and as a result, its value potential. Margaret Keane became famous in the 1960s and 1970s for her unnaturally doe-eyed children with expressionless faces. Nowadays, however, art collectors are more likely to think "Children of the Corn" than "I want that over my sofa."

This happens a lot with celebrity artists. Always be leery if an artist's fame is tied to something other than their artwork. A famous painter can live forever through their art. A famous vaudeville star? Not so much. Dealers had collectors lining up for comedian Red Skelton's clown art during the 1970s and 1980s. Now, unfortunately, most people don't even remember who Red Skelton was and clowns are considered creepy by many. (Thanks again, Stephen King!)

Don't get me wrong, if you see Ms. Keane's or Mr. Skelton's artwork at a swap meet, consider it, but understand that it will probably sell for far less than what galleries were selling it for thirty to forty years ago. Is the same fate in store for Thomas Kinkade's Keebler Elf cottages and actor Tony Curtis' Picasso-esque paintings of cats? Probably.

The "Knows" and "No's" of Picking
(or "Picking your Knows")

Once you've identified an intriguing piece in the field, it's time to take the next step: finding out as much as you can about it, negotiating a price, and closing the deal.

Here are some pre-purchase steps you'll want to consider:

Ask Questions:
Verbal testimony from a homeowner conducting a garage sale or a shopkeeper at an antique mall may be unreliable, but that doesn't mean you shouldn't ask questions. Even a simple "Where did this come from?" may give you important clues about a particular work's age and provenance.

Negotiate:
My Father is a great negotiator. Whenever I would fret about haggling on the price of something, my Father would always tell me: "The worst thing they can say is, 'no'". It's true. As someone who has been on the receiving end of a negotiating client, I can confirm that "no" is the worst thing I've ever said to them. (Ok, maybe "hell, no!") However, I've never thrown them out of my business.

That's not to say it's easy. Unlike some cultures, haggling isn't a tradition in America. As part of polite society we worry about offending, or appearing ignorant or greedy. However, negotiating is here to stay—especially in the picking realm—

and those who don't do it will be left behind (especially as more and more shops inflate their prices to allow them more wiggle-room in negotiations). Certainly don't lowball every offer (you want to be a welcome client, not a resented one), but it's fine to ask for a discount, especially if you're paying with cash or there are uncertainties with the piece.

Be the First one to Make an Offer

Studies have indicated that an item's ultimate sales price will be lower if the buyer makes the first offer. I've worked both sides, buyer and seller, and I can tell you that "Will you take $100 for this?" is far better than "Would you take less for this?" Being definitive tells the seller you're serious, and establishes a baseline for negotiations. Of course, if you make an offer, be prepared to pay it if it's accepted. Nothing will sour a seller quicker than your reneging on a verbal offer.

Terms of the Sale

"As is" and "all sales final" are phrases you'll be hearing quite a bit as a picker. After all, you'll be buying from pawn shops and garage sales, not Walmart. Still, if you're nervous that a piece may not be what it's purported to be, ask for a little time to check it out and the ability to return it if it's not (much like running a used car by a mechanic). That doesn't mean you should return it if it isn't as valuable as you thought/hoped it would be, but if you buy something under the auspices that it's an original oil painting, and it turns out to be an embellished giclee, then you should definitely be able to return it for a refund.

Please Note:

Just because an artwork is represented erroneously, doesn't mean that it was done intentionally. As we've discussed, art identification takes an educated eye, so don't necessarily accuse an errant seller of scamming. Return the item, accept their apologies … then recommend they pick-up a copy of *The Pocket Picker!*

Don't Be Afraid To Walk Away

There are a million opportunities out there, and another one is waiting right around the corner. That's easier said than done, especially if you're just getting your feet wet as a picker. Try to stay even keeled as you negotiate a price, bid on an item, or take time to do research. Don't let spinning dollar signs blind you to potential problems with a piece. If you feel queasy about a deal, then you probably shouldn't do it.

Picking Your Way
(What to do After Purchasing)

The Value Pyramid is all about helping you to make snap judgments about an artwork's potential value in the field. Once you get it home; however, you can delve much deeper into its value potential. Appraising an artwork is all about analyzing it against "comparables": other artworks with similar value characteristics. "Value characteristics" refer to a work's size, condition, period, medium, style, subject matter, history, or any other characteristic of the artwork that could, conceivably, impact its value positively or negatively. Whenever possible, you want to compare your pick against works with as many matching value characteristics as possible. You've heard the expression "comparing apples to apples"? This is it.

As an appraiser, this entails scouring auction records, inquiring to galleries and dealers, and poring over secondary market catalogues and artists' catalogue raisonnes. As a picker, you won't need (or want) that same level of due diligence; however, a bit of research and maybe a phone call can help determine if the next stop for your pick should be Sotheby's or The Salvation Army.

The first thing you'll want to do when you get home is to verify the value characteristics of your purchase. That means confirming, to the best of your ability, things like media, artist, condition, and authenticity. In the field, you'll likely have very limited access to the piece, but now it's yours to inspect and research at your leisure. This book, and your own experience, will assist you in making educated picks on-site, but the news won't always be good once you get serious about evaluating your find. You may find that "Lichtenstein" painting you bought at auction was by a "<u>starving artist</u>" named Gertrude rather than the world-famous Roy, or that the Rembrandt <u>etching</u> you stiff-armed people away from at the swap meet was trimmed and glued into the frame. Take a deep breath, sigh, and realize you're going to make the occasional bad pick no matter how careful and diligent you are. Conversely, there's no better feeling than getting an item home and realizing it was exactly what you hoped it was—and nobody else was wise enough to realize it!

As long as you exercise common sense when you examine your picks—i.e., don't handle <u>prints</u> after eating peanut butter and jelly, set heavy <u>sculpture</u> atop pictures framed in glass, lay paintings in the yard next to the sprinkler heads for inspection, etc.—you're probably going to be OK. However, you may want to consider wearing gloves, as the oils and dirt on our fingers can damage art over time. If your hands are going to be directly touching the delicate surface of the art or its <u>support</u>, then 100% cotton gloves are best; however, if you're moving framed art around, then clean rubber or workman gloves may work best. Use whatever will help you to keep a firm grip and protect your hands from frayed hanging wires and splintered wood frames.

With <u>original oils</u> and <u>acrylics</u>, you'll want to thoroughly inspect the materials and the work's backside (<u>verso</u>). If there's a paper dust cover backing, remove it. Often times, titles, signatures, dates, and other important information can be found on the back. There also may be a <u>gallery</u> certification or stamp that could provide clues about the work and its origin. Keep in mind that writing on the wood stretcher bars of the fram-

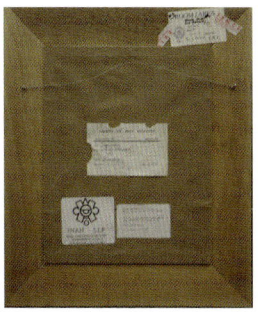

The verso of this work is chock-full of useful information.

ing is often placed by the gallery or frame shop that framed the piece, and may reference the work's inventory number or a particular type of moulding or frame style. This information is less useful than writing on the <u>canvas</u> itself, which is typically applied by the artist and is more likely to reference the art and the art alone.

Even if there is no writing, stamps, stickers or information of any kind on the back, the framing materials will provide information about a work. Are nails used? Staples? Glue? If the canvas is affixed to the stretcher bars using nails, it is more likely to be an antique than one affixed using staples. Similarly, if the corners of the stretcher bars are joined using nails, it's probably much older than those joined with hinges, wedges and wood glue. Of course, old canvases may be stretched on modern materials (and vice versa), so don't look at the age of framing materials as a telltale sign, but rather one of the many important clues you'll gather to solve the mystery of your pick.

You probably won't need to physically remove a painting on canvas or board entirely from its frame; however, it may be necessary if you're still uncertain if a particular work is a painting or a print. If it is a print, the border of the work (which is usually obscured by the frame) will be uniform around all four edges of the piece. On a hand-painted piece, you'll often find paint splattered along the edges of the stretched canvas (painting is a messy business), and the work's borders will not be symmetrical.

Since the majority of damage in vintage works on paper comes from what was originally intended to protect it—its framing—you may want to remove it entirely. Techniques for framing oil paintings have remained largely unchanged for hundreds of years; however, 18th century framers had neither the materials nor inclination to properly preserve prints. While paintings could be valuable, most prints of the time (etchings, stone lithography, etc.) were considered purely decorative and treated as such. The 20th century ushered in developments in cotton rag matting, UV (ultraviolet) glass and acid-free foam boards, but these materials didn't become commonplace at neighborhood frame shops until the 1980s. As a result, the vast majority of framing you'll encounter is hurting the art more than helping—both from a value and preservation standpoint.

Become friends with a good local framer with knowledge of museum-quality conservational materials. You'll be seeing them a lot. I know what you're thinking—"Great, more expense." Not necessarily. The knowledge you'll glean about your works, and the conservation a professional framer can provide, will offset the expense in the long run.

As a profiteering picker, you probably don't want to hear about the I.R.S., but when it comes to perusing and protecting your paper picks I recommend it:

1. Inspect:

Have a trusted framer look the piece over. If the presentation is conservational (and doesn't make the piece look hideous), then leave it as is. If not, then …

2. Remove:

The condition will only get worse within a bad environment, and removing it from the frame will reveal any and all damage the print may have sustained. (Many collectors of vintage prints prefer them to be unframed for that very reason.) Ask your framer if you can observe the extraction process and the tools involved, as you'll eventually want to tackle the removal of some artworks yourself. (Make sure you practice on the cheapies!)

3. Secure:

After you know all the facts about the condition of your piece, then you can make an educated decision about how to best protect it. This can be done in a number of ways: retrofitting the existing frame with conservational components (such as rag matting and acid-free backing board), keeping the piece unframed and placing it within a protective sleeve or portfolio; or completely reframing the work in contemporary moulding and museum quality materials.

If you replace a frame, and are concerned that it could have value—keep it. There's no reason to keep an artwork in an ugly, dated, non-conservational frame, but that doesn't mean you have to throw it out. If you're unsure, ask your framer—they should be able to tell mass-produced or "ready-made" moulding from that which has been carefully crafted.

Once you've secured your pick and gleaned as much physical information about it as you can, it's time to put on your detective cap and do a little digging. In most cases, to borrow the tagline from my favorite science fiction show growing up,

"The Truth is Out There." You just need to know where to look. Sometimes a quick Internet search will tell you everything you need to know about an artwork; sometimes you'll need to track down experts and spend time in the library scouring texts.

Three years ago, I was presented with a mold purportedly derived from a 500 year-old beeswax sculpture hand-carved by Leonardo da Vinci. Gulp! Needless to say, you don't get any higher up the "Value Pyramid" than ol' Leonardo. His artworks, which include Mona Lisa and The Last Supper, are history's most revered and analyzed. They are also ridiculously rare. Fewer than twenty paintings in the world have been directly attributed to Leonardo, and all are housed in prestigious museums. Even Bill Gates, Microsoft's Chairman and billionaire, had to "settle" for one of Leonardo's scientific journals, which he purchased for $30 Million in 1994.

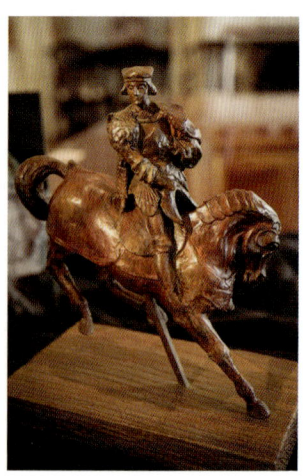

As an appraiser, I've been privileged to appraise original works by Masters like Pablo Picasso, Diego Rivera, Salvador Dali, Thomas Moran and Alberto Giacometti, but I never, ever, expected to be approached with an artwork from history's ultimate Renaissance Man. It was only after nearly two years of research—verifying expert testimony, documenting the

"Horse and Rider."
Leonardo da Vinci.
Circa 1508.

work's inclusion in historical texts, and tracing its half-a-millennium provenance—that we felt confident unveiling the sculpture, dubbed "Horse and Rider," to the world in 2012.

Chances are you won't have to work that hard. Researching an artwork has been made infinitely easier by the 21st century resources at our disposal. Twenty years ago, appraisers needed to live at the library and could potentially spend thousands of dollars accumulating <u>catalogue raissones</u>, biographies and auction catalogues. Most of that information in now accessible with a few strokes of the keyboard, and a surprising amount may be gleaned for free.

As a certified appraiser, I've used thousands of resources over the years. As a picker, you won't need or want that many; however, you'll want a handful that provide a wide range of information that crosses all genres of art. Here are a few that you may want to lean on:

www.askart.com:

A modest fee is required to access auction results on this site; however, there is no charge to access the site's sizeable database of listed artists. This is handy if you want to check to see if the artist of an artwork you discovered is of any repute. This can also help if a portion of a signature is illegible. Many times I've been able to extrapolate an artist's name based on a few letters by searching alphabetically and utilizing the process of elimination. It is also useful from a resale standpoint, as it identifies the auction houses, dealers, and museums who routinely handle these artists.

www.artvalue.com:

I pay to access askart.com's auction database, but this one is free and I probably use it more. It features a greater number of International artists, and its scope of auction results includes graphic works (prints), whereas askart.com does not.

www.google.com:

Shhh, don't tell anyone, but this appraiser "Googles" all the time. Sure, it'll send you on a fair share of wild goose chases, but it can also lead you to artist's biographies, auction records, and a nearly infinite list of dealers, galleries and museums. Additionally, its "spell check" on searches (which is based on how often a particular word is searched for and how many results it garners) can sometimes identify your artist when you can't. Make sure you add words like "artist" or "painting" to your search in order to distinguish the artist from that Brazilian porn star they share a name with.

www.artprice.net:

When you first visit this excellent site, be sure to sign-up for their free Art Market Insight's newsletter which is sent via e-mail. Just like a day trader needs to understand trends in the stock market if they want to excel, you'll want to understand current trends in the art market. It's an excellent resource—one that I often quote in my own reports.

www.artistssignatures.com:

Esteemed art researcher, John Castagno, has published twelve comprehensive signature directories over the past twenty years. Most are still available through Amazon.com—for a couple hundred dollars apiece. That may be a bargain if you're an appraiser, authenticator or historian, but if you're a picker you may want to stick to the $10/month or pay-as-you-need online version.

Hislop's Official International Price Guide to Fine Art

As an appraiser, I don't use price guides in my evaluations … but that doesn't mean you shouldn't! Like askart.com, Hislop's lists most esteemed National and International artists, and its printed form makes it more useful in the field. Its listed price ranges are often comically broad without context (oil paintings by Andy Warhol are listed for between $2,500 and $8,500,000), but it will still help you to identify the value potential for desirable artists.

Picking Up the Phone

In some cases, you're going to want to call in the Cavalry and solicit help with your pick. Successful picking is contingent upon maximizing profits, and keeping expenses down is an important part of that; however, at a certain point, trying to do-it-yourself will cost you time, money and profits. We've already talked about the importance of fostering a relationship with a good framer, but there will be times you're going to need the services of museum curators, conservators, authenticators and, yes, even appraisers like myself.

Don't be intimidated to contact these folks and, don't worry, the meter doesn't start running the minute they pick-up the phone. A thoughtfully posed inquiry can often shed light on your pick without spending a cent. For example, you might approach a museum curator with the following query: "Excuse me, sir/madam, but I believe I have discovered an original work by an artist housed in your museum. How can I go about determining its authenticity?" They may offer to help you directly, or they may recommend someone to you, but either way you know more than you did.

Remember, however, that these are professionals, who put many years into education and plying their trade, and that will be reflected by a professional (i.e., expensive) hourly rate. ("Do you charge for appraisals?" is right up there with "You ever hear of an artist named _____?" as my favorite opening questions from prospective clients.) Don't waste their time and, if they advise you, be prepared to compensate them. A professional may be able to tell in thirty seconds what would take you weeks of research, so do everything possible to keep these people in your corner:

1. Museum Curators:

A search of a database like askart.com, or even a simple Google search, will often reveal museums that house work by the artist you're investigating. Curators are the people who oversee, direct and administrate these museums and their collections. Most curators know the artists in their museum backwards and forwards, and therefore, can be a valuable resource (especially since works housed in prestigious museum collections often must be appraised, authenticated and restored). Keep in mind, however, that unlike the other professionals listed below, Curators aren't paid to be consultants to the general public. Be especially respectful and mindful of their time.

2. Appraisers:

Art appraisers certified through a recognized entity (ISA and ASA are the biggies) can help in innumerable ways. If you're confident in the authenticity and value potential of what you have, a written and certified appraisal report can assist you in the works' resale and the procurement of

Brett Says: "www.appraisers.org is the website for the American Society of Appraisers. Its 'find an appraiser' feature can help you to find an appraiser in your area."

appropriate insurance (something you'll need if you're jetting the piece to a gallery or auction house). They can also help to fill-in the gaps in your own research and help you to formulate a specific plan for your pick. Many appraisers, like myself, make themselves available for verbal consultations which can be invaluable for identification and estimating value potential.

3. Conservators:

I recommend resisting the temptation to clean, touch-up, or otherwise restore artwork yourself. Dabbing that area of missing black paint with a Sharpee pen may seem innocuous, and may even make the art look better, but you just hurt its value and your ability to resell it. Cleaning and touch-up of art and framing by professionals isn't all that expensive, and there's no way you want to attempt major <u>restoration</u> (such as patching a <u>canvas</u>, or repainting areas of loss) on a valuable piece. If you do feel compelled to experiment with cleaning and touch-up, there are all kinds of "Do-it-yourself" guides out there—just make sure you practice on a pick you swung and missed on.

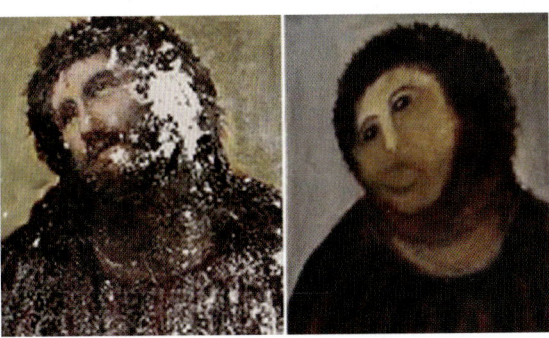

*Uh-Oh! This is what can happen
when you don't use a professional conservator.*

4. Authenticators:

Authentication of <u>prints</u> and <u>originals</u> by emerging and mid-tier artists probably isn't necessary. For the same reason counterfeiters typically don't bother counterfeiting $1 bills, it doesn't make sense for a criminal to forge art by artists whose works sell for nominal amounts. Works by "<u>Art 101</u> artists" will likely need authentication; however, the chances of authenticating a Monet painting discovered at a swap meet are slim. As our society has become more litigious, fewer experts are willing to put their necks on the line to proclaim unknown works as authentic, and as you climb higher up the value pyramid, fewer recognized experts exist (and their rates can be exorbitant).

"If/Then" Logic:

Before engaging the services of any fine art professional, I recommend using the "if/then" test to determine the cost effectiveness of doing so. Philosophy in picking? You better believe it! Applying "if/then" logic (i.e., IF all politicians lie and Carol is a politician, THEN Carol is a liar) can help you to determine if a piece of art is worth the trouble and expense. Basically, it boils down to this: "if" a service adds more value to the work than the expense, "then" it's probably worth doing. If spending a couple hundred dollars to replace that horribly dated 1960s frame will enable you to resell the work quicker and for a higher amount, then do it! If it will cost $5,000 to restore an oil painting worth $3,000 in good condition, then don't!

The "if/then" test can be particularly handy when it comes to authentication. Remember that Andy Warhol sketch I mentioned earlier? It depicted famous 1930s crooner Rudy Vallee, was purchased from a Las Vegas estate sale for $5, and was appraised in 2011, by yours truly, for over two million dollars. It generated a lot of buzz and proved quite controversial, but I don't doubt its authenticity. Why? The "if/then" test.

A little background—the work was purchased from an estate with ties to Andy Warhol. (The seller's Aunt had worked for the Warhol family and helped Andy convalesce from Chorea when he was a child.) The sketch itself was hidden amongst drawings by another artist, and the purchaser didn't discover it until the drawing it was behind was removed from its frame. The crudely rendered portrait depicted famous 1930s crooner Rudy Vallee, a childhood idol of Warhols, who he would frequently listen to on the radio as a sick child confined to his bedroom.

Before taking the assignment of appraising it, I put the piece to the "if/then" test: IF it wasn't an authentic Andy Warhol drawing, THEN what was it? My answer: one of the most elaborate—and elaborately idiotic—art hoaxes of all-time. Forgeries and knock-offs of Warhols' famous 1960s era Pop Art are common, but why would someone forge one of his unrefined childhood sketches and then hide it away from the world for decades? My answer: they wouldn't.

Of course, there was other evidence (the signature, additional history, stylistic hallmarks, etc.) that further convinced me, but that was the gist of the "if/then" test in that instance. A positive "if/then" test may not be enough to ensure an authenticator will sign-off on a work as authentic, but it may help you to determine whether or not to procure their services.

One last word about utilizing the services of fine art professionals—the higher the potential value of a piece, the higher the standards of expertise. Your local frame shop may do a fine job cleaning a contemporary oil painting, but don't ask them to restore a Renoir. Similarly, a regional art dealer may be just fine for authenticating signed and numbered lithographs, but don't expect their opinion to hold weight on a potential Picasso.

Picking and Grinning
(Selling your Picks for Profit)

Once you've reviewed your picking purchase and have a pretty good idea of what it is, its condition, authenticity and potential value, it's time to work towards the ultimate goal: selling it for profit.

Ideally, when you sell a pick, you'll want to get as close to its "Fair Market Value" as possible. Fair Market Value is defined as the price at which buyers and sellers with a reasonable knowledge of pertinent facts and not acting under any compulsion are willing to do business.

In order for a particular art piece to recognize its full Fair Market Value potential, it must be presented to a knowledgeable buyer within a market, and market level, appropriate to the piece. This is referred to as the property's "Highest and Best Use." Is selling a Picasso at a swap meet indicative of its Highest and Best Use? Of course not. That's why most news stories of found masterpieces begin at garage sales and end at International art auctions like Sotheby's or Christie's.

Most of your finds, even the best ones, won't be news-worthy. Successful picking is simply a matter of rescuing an artwork from an inappropriate market, and selling it within one more conducive to its worth. Even if, for whatever reason, you're forced to sell a piece at a market level similar to the one from which it was purchased (garage sale to eBay, for example), your ability to enhance the work—through identification, provenance, presentation, etc—will add to its desirability and keep you from incurring a financial loss in most cases.

Highest and Best Use of an Art Object is Primarily Dictated by Three Factors

1. Subject Matter:

This is largely common sense. Southwestern and Native American art is more likely to sell through <u>galleries</u> and <u>dealers</u> in the Southwestern US, than through those in New York or overseas. Conversely, you wouldn't go to rural Oklahoma to sell a bustling Manhattan cityscape. Knowing your audience is key to being a successful picker. For example, if you only buy and sell locally, you might think twice about picking duck stamp prints in the Las Vegas desert.

2. Artist:

Similarly, many artists are more popular and collectible in certain areas of the country or the world. Western artist Jack White was the Official Artist of Texas and the Great Grand-son of Texas Ranger, Ben McGee. I'll give you three guesses as to where his work is most marketable.

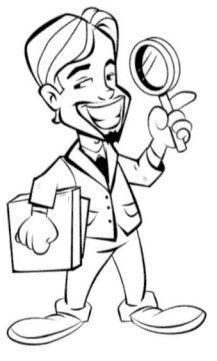

Brett Says: "Remember, in order to achieve highest value, a piece must be thoroughly indicative of the style and subject matter for which the artist is renowned.

If an artist is known for their abstracts, don't expect a realistic work to approach the same value."

3. Potential Value:

Most "<u>Art 101</u>" artists we've discussed (Picasso, Renoir, Van Gogh, etc.) transcend regionality to a large degree, and where to place the work should largely be dictated by an artwork's potential value. An art dealer in Cleveland may be a fine choice to help you sell a graphic work by Joan Miro, but one of his original paintings would likely be more at home, and sell for a higher value, through a high-end International auction house like Sotheby's or Christie's. The higher up the value spectrum, the more likely you'll want to try to place the work through high-end art dealers, galleries and auction houses in New York, Los Angeles, or such International meccas for fine art collectors as London, Paris and, more recently, Tokyo and Dubai.

In a perfect world, you'd present your find directly to a stable of collectors ready and willing to pay you Fair Market Value in full (and in cash, of course!). That doesn't happen often. Instead, you'll most often be dealing with art galleries, dealers, auction houses and other secondary market sources that don't purchase directly and throw around terms like "consignment," "brokerage" and "commission."

Art Galleries

Art galleries provide a brick and mortar location and, hopefully, professional presentation and a steady stream of prospective clients. Most galleries won't purchase artwork from you outright, but may agree to consign it (to display it for a certain period of time), and sell it on commission (an agreed upon percentage of its ultimate sale price). Consignment agreements may last from a few weeks to several years, and commission rates could vary from 25-50%. "50%!?!" I hear you scream. That may sound high, but if a gallery is able to market your art, professionally present it to established collectors, and sell it for amounts far in excess of what you could sell it for on your own, then it may be the best contract you ever signed.

Still, these agreements aren't to be entered into lightly. First of all, you should make sure the gallery is appropriate and reputable. Place a work in an inappropriate venue and it may be in purgatory for the duration of the contract. Once you've agreed to allow a gallery to consign or broker your art, it's theirs, for all intents and purposes, until the contract expires. You won't be able to market it on your own, and you may be out of luck should a better opportunity or venue for the work come available while you're under contract. Even worse, your art could be damaged or stolen. Search the Internet and you'll find hundreds of stories of disreputable galleries mishandling art, or closing overnight and absconding with their inventory.

Don't let a few bad apples spoil the bunch, however. Most galleries are legitimate, and work diligently to sell their inventory. Potential concerns can be alleviated by closely reading any contracts and asking appropriate questions. For Example: Do they have insurance? What do they do to promote their art? How soon after the sale can you expect payment? Etc. For high value works, you may want to consult with an attorney before committing.

Hold galleries you work with long distance to an even higher standard. It's one thing if you can drop in on a local gallery to ensure your art is being marketed and presented properly (or being presented at all), but another if an out-of-state gallery you can't monitor has your art. Additionally, shipping of fine art is always a risky proposition (see page 95 for tips on shipping).

Finding appropriate galleries is often as simple as searching for them on the Internet. Google the artist's name, then add words like "gallery" or "dealer" to your search. Websites like www.askart.com also list "Blue Book" dealers and galleries for particular listed artists. If you can't find resources for your specific artist, or if the artist is unknown, try looking for dealers of the work's genre, period or subject matter (i.e., "Southwestern Prints," "Antique Etchings," "Renaissance Paintings," etc.). Always try to place your picks through sources well-versed in the marketing of comparable art, as they'll likely have the knowledge and client base necessary to sell them expeditiously and for appropriate values.

Auctions

Unless you're talking about established auction houses like Christie's and Sotheby's, auction results can be fickle. A bad storm during a regional auction could limit attendance and cause a valuable artwork to sell for a fraction of its expected price. That's great if you're a storm-braving picker; not so great if you're the poor schlub who consigned the piece.

For that reason, I encourage extreme caution when reselling art through auction houses. Most regional auction houses lack the connoisseurship and client base necessary to sell fine art effectively and for appropriate values. They deal with a hodgepodge of personal property, from jewelry to garden gnomes, and are usually more concerned with sales volume than optimizing the values met for specific items.

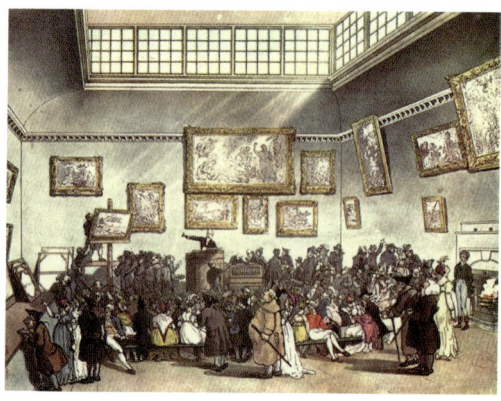

Prestigious auction houses like Christie's and Sotheby's have auctioned fine artwork for over 250 years.

As when dealing with prospective galleries, ask plenty of questions. Ask about their fine art acumen, attendance, and most importantly, ask if they allow a "reserve" (a predetermined amount an item must reach at auction in order for it to sell). <u>Auction houses</u> only get paid if an item sells, so most frown on reserves, or try to set them as low as possible. As the seller, however, it may be the only protection you have if the auction is unsuccessful.

If you have a piece you suspect is worth more than $10,000, you'll probably want to consider high-end International auction houses like Christie's, Sotheby's and Bonham's. You won't have to worry about their ability to attract buyers, and each one has "in-house" appraisers, <u>conservators</u>, and authenticators, which can help streamline the process for consigners.

Unfortunately, this added expertise comes with higher

commission rates and buyer's premiums … and no guarantees. You'll also want to make sure the piece will be featured in an appropriate and timely auction. Unlike some regional auction houses, Sotheby's doesn't have auctions every weekend, and most are "themed" (i.e., "20th Century Modern," "Works of the Renaissance," etc.). It may take months, or even years, for them to have an auction with a theme appropriate for your piece.

Museums

This is for higher-end art, obviously. You're not going to find many museums interested in your beat-up Renoir poster. However, museums purchase more than you might think. Many have yearly procurement budgets to augment their collection of donated and lent works.

Of course, museums don't tend to gamble on works picked from garage sales, so make sure any work you submit for consideration has been analyzed by a professional. A certified appraisal or authentication will hold weight with most museums—your Internet analysis of the signature probably won't.

Even if a museum doesn't purchase, you may want to consider lending, or even donating the piece to them. That Andy Warhol I appraised was eventually placed on loan at Bristol's prestigious Royal West of England Academy, where it was seen by thousands of people. That exhibition is now part of the work's provenance, which, as we've discussed, can be an important contributor to value. Another important consideration is this—you're not storing it! Which is a better environment for a valuable piece of art: well displayed and adequately insured on the wall of a prominent museum? Or under your bed?

Donating a piece to a museum may not provide the cash windfall you hoped, but in many circumstances you can write-off its full Fair Market Value for tax purposes (with a certified appraisal, of course). It's also a nice feeling to know you contributed to a museum's utility. Who knows? You might even get your name on a placard or in a program.

Online

Online auctions and brokers have their advantages—the commission percentages are usually lower than "brick-and-mortar" galleries, and you won't have to give-up the inventory until a sale has been consummated. That's a nice feeling. On the other hand, this market level is rife with fraud, either intentionally through scammers looking to make a quick buck, or unintentionally through uneducated sellers not knowing what they have. It's nearly impossible to be certain of an artwork's condition, quality and authenticity from a postage-stamp sized picture and a few glamorized words from the seller. Add to that an iffy-at-best return policy and you probably won't find many serious collectors shopping for art online.

I'd resist the temptation of using it as a dumping ground for crap, too. If you made a bad pick of a termite-ridden old poster, don't try to get your money back selling it to some unwary eBay bidder in Tuscaloosa. Throw it away or donate it, but don't risk your reputation glorifying refuse.

The online route works best for "fringe" works—ones that have value, but not so much so that you should spend hours and hours trying to sell it. Vintage prints by mid-tier artists are perfect for this. If you can take that $5 mystery print from the swap meet and accurately attribute it to a prominent 19th century engraver, then you may be able to sell it online for a few hundred dollars. Not bad!

How to Transport Art

Don't ship artwork with glass. Glass is heavy (so your shipment will be more expensive) and breaks easily. Rest assured, if the glass breaks in transit your investment will be ruined. Either remove the glass, replace it with Plexiglas (or a comparable acrylic), or ship the work unframed. If you absolutely, positively have to ship a work with glass, place masking tape across its entire surface. That way, if the glass does break, the tape may keep it in place.

Also, avoid using tubes whenever possible. Tubes are convenient and may be suitable for posters and inexpensive prints, but they aren't appropriate for fine art. Rolling can cause cracking in oils on canvas, creasing in works paper, and unless you know what you're doing, an artwork can easily be damaged during placement and removal. Shipping flat keeps the art in its intended state and, if done properly, reduces its risk of damage. Consult with a reputable shipper of fine art on how to best ship your item flat.

Pick-adilloes
(Common Picking Pitfalls)

Earlier in this book, I said that successful picking entails taking advantage of other people's ignorance. That doesn't mean you should throw ethics and scruples out the window. It's one thing to skillfully identify an important detail an unwary seller might have missed; it's another to intentionally deceive or take advantage of someone.

It's an easy trap to fall into, and one of many pitfalls you'll want to avoid as a picker. Regardless of how you market your picks, or the market level you utilize to do so, there are certain guidelines you should adhere to in order to ensure your long-term success:

Be Truthful

Knowledge can be a double-edged sword. It can help you to find a diamond in a mountain of coal, but what if you learn the diamond is just glass? If research shows that Dali you hoped was authentic is, in fact, a fake, don't try to sell it as anything but. Avoid errors of omission, too. Being intentionally vague about a work in order to gloss over or minimize its potential defects is almost as bad as fudging a signature on an unsigned piece.

Don't be Greedy

You don't want to get taken, but your goal shouldn't be to take someone else either. Offer a fair price and an honest assessment of your finds, and people will want to work with you again and again. Overprice your items and fudge their descriptions, and soon you'll be as popular as a velvet Elvis at the Louvre.

Never Dismiss the Path of Least Resistance

Variations of this statement have been made to me numerous times over the years: "I took this artwork I bought at the Swap Meet for $5 to XYZ Gallery/Dealer/Broker, and they offered me $100 for it. That's when I knew I had something valuable, and they were trying to screw me!" Not necessarily. Yes, it probably means you have a piece worth in excess of the $5 you paid for it, but it doesn't necessarily mean they were "trying to screw you" (anymore than you were "trying to screw" the guy you bought it from at the swap meet). They likely knew there was value to the piece, but they also realized they would have to advertise it, clean it, frame it, authenticate it, display it, appraise it, and any number of other steps that may be essential to its resale. They've got a business to run, and NO business can survive paying Fair Market Value out-of-pocket (before expenses) in order to resell it.

I may not have said so at the time, but in many of those cases the client would have been better off taking the offer. Think about it: selling a work for $100 that you purchased for $5 is a 1,900% profit! That's impressive. Could you milk a higher profit margin over time? Possibly, but then you'd be out time and many of the same expenses XYZ Gallery/Dealer/ Broker would have been saddled with had you accepted their offer. That doesn't mean you should take the first profitable offer that comes down the pike in every circumstance (if you follow the guidelines of this book, you should have a reasonable idea of what you have and its value potential going in), but don't dismiss making a tidy profit with the least amount of fuss and muss.

Don't Be Afraid to Make a Mistake

This isn't brain surgery, or the day-trading of blue-chip stocks. As a picker, you're rarely going to know all the facts about a piece, so the occasional bad purchase is inevitable. Don't let it deter you. In fact, you should embrace them. If you spend $20 on a worthless piece, but learn why it's worthless and are able to avoid making the same mistake in the future, then it was money well spent.

Be Prepared For When Your Work Doesn't Sell

Sometimes you'll have trouble selling even your best picks. Don't get discouraged. If you follow the advice and guidelines laid out in this book, the art you purchased will more than likely gain value over time, so don't fret if you can't sell it immediately. Not everyone collects art. Even rare pieces by Masters can take time to find an appropriate home.

Unfortunately, this can create a back-log of art that will need to be properly preserved and stored in the interim. People always ask me: "Brett, what's the safest place to store art?" "On the wall," I reply. That's not me being flippant, smart-alecky art guy; that's me being honest. Bad things are far more likely to happen to art stuffed into your closet, garage, or some storage unit, than it is on your wall. Besides, art was meant to be seen, and that can't happen if it's gathering dust in the attic.

When hanging antique art, always be mindful of the hanging apparatus. Just like us, wire gets brittle as it ages. It can break, sending that rare 19th century Hudson River School painting crashing to the ground face-first (paintings ALWAYS crash face-first). Double-check the wire, the screw eyes (the circular screws the wire is affixed to), and the frame itself, to make sure everything is sturdily fastened and secure. If it's not, then replace it. This is not where you want to pinch-pennies. These are cheap fixes that will protect your investment.

Once the work is secure on the wall, you can get to the best part—enjoying it! Even if it's a piece you don't plan to keep or even particularly like, hanging it for display will allow you to bask in the glory of your find like the proud picker you are!

Of course, if you REALLY despise the work, or run out of wall space, or don't want that Vargas' nude hanging in little Joey's room, you may be forced to store your artwork at some point. When you do, here are my recommendations:

Keep it out of sunlight.

This may be common sense, but in Las Vegas I see so much sun-damaged art (usually brought in by sun-damaged owners) that it bears repeating. Artworks, especially those on paper, are extremely susceptible to the effects of direct sunlight. I've seen colors wash-out and signatures fade into oblivion after only a few years of hanging in a sunny spot. Even indirect sunlight (i.e., reflective light) can damage an artwork over time. UV glass or acrylic, installed over your artwork or windows, can mitigate or eliminate sunlight's damage potential.

Make sure its climate controlled.

Art isn't some delicate flower that will wilt the moment conditions aren't right, but it does need a relatively consistent environment to survive and thrive over long periods. Drastic temperature and climate changes are the biggest threat, and can result in everything from warping of the frame and stretcher bars, to mold and mildew developing on the art itself. Cool and dry is best, but consistency is key.

Don't roll it!

If you have unframed prints, posters or canvas paintings, the temptation is to roll them, tube them, and forget about them. Avoid that temptation. Rolling an item for short term storage or transport is probably fine, but I'd discourage anything longer than a few weeks. Rolling a canvas painting that's the slightest bit wet can be disastrous, and even one that's totally cured can develop abrasions and surface cracquelure over time. Works on paper are easily dented and have a "memory" when rolled for extended periods, making them difficult to flatten and their ultimate preservation and framing difficult. Add to that the non-conservational nature of most tubes, and rolled storage is something to avoid whenever possible.

Always store unframed art flat, off the ground on a sturdy shelf or table, and preferably in its own portfolio case. You can typically stack like-art (canvas on canvas, paper prints on paper prints, etc.), but you'll probably want to place an acid-free barrier sheet between each one. Conversely, you should NEV-ER store framed art flat. Storing framed art vertically increases accessibility and reduces your risk of damage. Position them upright, back-to-back and face-to-face. (You never want the back of one painting placed against the front of another, as the frame and hanging apparatuses can damage the surface of a work.) Whenever possible, place a piece of cardboard, foam-board, or the like between them as a barrier. As with prints, try to keep them off the ground whenever possible. Even a few inches can protect paintings from a busted water heater or insect invasion. Heavy shelving or a covered wood pallet should do the trick.

Know When to Fold 'Em

If you make a bad pick, it's best to cut ties with it ASAP. Twenty years from now, a piece of crap is still going to be a piece of crap. Don't make a bad situation worse by wasting storage space on it, or trying to pawn it off on another poor sap. Swallow your pride, admit your mistake, and donate it to Goodwill.

Sometimes you may even want to throw in the towel on a decent piece. "Sloppy Seconds" is a vulgar term, but it's applicable in the art world. If your piece of art has "been around the block a few times" (such as multiple appearances at auction in a short period of time) it will lose value and few collectors will touch it. At that point, your options are to cut and run, or stick it back in storage until the market changes.

Peter Picked
a Pack of Pollock Paintings
(A Few Final Words …)

I want to end by discussing the most crucial element for successful picking: YOU. A good mechanic needs good tools, but good tools don't necessarily make for a good mechanic. *The Pocket Picker* is a tool—hopefully, a good one—but it is no substitute for your own eyes, intuition, and connoisseurship.

As you develop your picking skills, I encourage you to focus on inexpensive picks from a genre, style or media that you enjoy. Not only will that make picking more fun—especially as you work towards the "money making" stage—but will speed your learning curve. Get a kick out of exploring an artist's psyche? Pick some <u>Abstract</u>, Surreal or Expressionist artworks. Like history? Look for allegorical or genre scenes. Religious? There are plenty of icons and biblical works to pick from.

Once you've had a few hits, however, swing for the fences on a few picks "outside the zone". Challenging yourself will keep things fresh, improve your abilities and, most importantly, help you to thrive as markets, styles and tastes change. As I trained to become an appraiser, my instructors told me that I shouldn't expect a client to pay for my education—meaning I shouldn't charge my customers for time spent learning and researching something I should already know. As a picker; however, you have no such constraints. Time spent researching and educating yourself on an unknown pick will influence its value potential and increase your profit margins.

As you proceed down the "Picking Path," please keep me posted on your progress. Nothing would make me happier than hearing how *The Pocket Picker* helped you to secure a valuable piece, so shoot me a letter or e-mail about your latest score or adventure (or misadventure!). And if you discover a particularly good tip that I might have missed, please let me know. Who knows? Maybe I'll feature it, and you, in the sequel!

Good luck and Happy Picking!

Sincerely,

Brett K. Maly
Brett@artencounter.com

Glossary

Abstract (right): Art that does not depict recognizable or realistic forms from the physical world.

Acid Burn: Discoloration caused by acid migrating onto the artwork, often from the matting or backing materials.

Acid Free: Often used to describe conservation grade board, paper or adhesive that has a neutral ph value of 7 or higher.

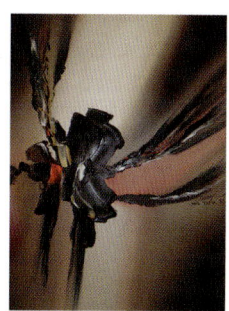

"Into the Night"
by Paul Tapia.

Acidic: In paper, an unstable state whereby the molecular structure of the paper breaks down, causing discoloration and weakening of the sheet.

Acrylic Paint: A fast-drying synthetic paint made from acrylic resin.

Aging: The action of atmospheric components, such as light and temperature, on materials and structures leading to deterioration over time.

Aquatint: A printmaking process of the intaglio family made to resemble a watercolor through the use of nitric acid and powdered rosin.

Art 101: For the purpose of this book, refers to artists that nearly everyone has heard of, regardless of their fine art knowledge or acumen.

Artist proof (A/P): A special edition of a print published for the artist's personal inspection, use, and possible sale.

Artist's Bluebook: A registry or directory of notable fine artists.

Auction House: A company that runs auctions where works are bid on and sold to collectors. International auction houses include Sotheby's, Christie's, and Bonham's.

Bevel: Edge that is cut obliquely on a slant. Can refer to any surface, but in art and framing most commonly refers to wood, matboard, and glass.

Block: The wooden element which is printed in making woodcuts and wood engraving. The word also applies to typographical printing elements.

Broker: An intermediary between artists and collectors, galleries, auction houses and museums.

Buckling: Shrinkage or waviness of a surface resulting from environmental action.

Canvas: An artistic support, primarily used in acrylic and oil painting, made from linen or cotton and stretched tightly across stretcher bars.

Catalogue Raisonnes: A comprehensive catalogue of artworks by an artist.

Certificate of Authenticity: A document attesting to the authenticity of an individual piece of art.

Composition: The arrangement of elements within the design area.

Commission: A fee paid to a broker, dealer, gallery, auction house or other entity for negotiating a sale. This fee is usually based on a percentage of the sale price.

Conservation: The preservation and protection of artwork to prevent damage caused by exposure to the elements.

Conservator: A person specially trained in the care, maintenance, and restoration of works of art.

Consignment: Placing artwork in the hands of another entity, such as a gallery or auction house, but retaining ownership until the items are sold.

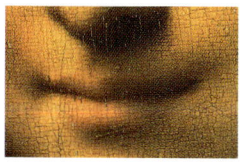

Craquelure (left): A system of cracks that develop in the surface of a painting due to environmental action (such as expansion and contraction) and/or the natural aging process of the artist's technique and materials.

Crayon: A stick of colored chalk or wax, used for drawing. Special crayons are also used in the production of stone lithography.

Dealer: A person or company that buys and sells works of art—usually of a specific genre, style or period.

Digital Prints: See Giclees.

Drawing: The act of representing an image on a surface by means of adding lines and shades, as with a pencil, crayon, pen, chalk, pastels, etc. Also refers to an illustration that has been drawn by hand.

Drypoint: A printmaking technique of the intaglio family, in which an image is incised onto a printing plate with a hard-pointed "needle" of sharp metal or diamond point.

Edition Size: The number of reproductions that total a given print or canvas release. The total number produced should not exceed the number represented.

Embellished: Some prints, especially those on canvas, can support brushstrokes added in post-production. If done well, and by the original artist, these additions can enhance both aesthetic and value.

Embossing: A printmaking method in which a design is impressed into paper, creating a heavily raised surface area.

Engraving: A printmaking process which uses incision as means of marking the design.

Épreuve d'artiste (E/A): French designation for Artist Proof.

Expressionism: An artistic movement originating in Germany at the beginning of the 20th century. It seeks to present the world in a subjective manner, distorting the physical world in order to evoke emotion or thought.

Etching: A print technique in which an impression of an image is taken (or "pulled") from a metallic plate etched through the use of acids.

Fair Market Value: Price at which property would change hands between a willing buyer and seller, when neither is forced to buy or sell, and when both have reasonable knowledge of all relevant facts.

Foxing/Fox Marks: Circular discolorations in paper believed to be caused by micro-organisms developing at high humidity. Non-conservational framing may cause or exacerbate this effect.

Foundry: A place in which metal castings are produced.

Foundry Mark: A mark or inscription on a sculpture, usually on its base, signifying the foundry from which it was cast.

Gallery: A showroom where works of art are exhibited and normally offered for purchase.

Gallery Wrap: Stretching an artist's canvas so that the canvas and composition wrap around the sides of the stretcher bars. This allows for a frameless presentation of the finished painting.

Giclee: A French word meaning "to squirt". In printmaking, it refers to a reproduction made using an inkjet printer.

Gouache: An opaque (non-transparent) watercolor.

Hand-Coloring: Watercolor or gouache coloring added to a print, either by the original artist or a studio artist, with either a brush or a stencil cut to allow uniform highlights to particular areas.

Hand-Embellished: See Embellished.

Highest and Best Use: The reasonable, probable, feasible, and legal use of a property that results in its highest value.

Hors De Commerce (H/C): A French term meaning "not for sale." Typically refers to a special edition of a print published for inspection, use, and possible sale by the artist, gallery or publisher.

Hudson River School: The first coherent school of American art; active from 1825 to 1870; painted wilderness landscapes of the Hudson River valley and surrounding New England.

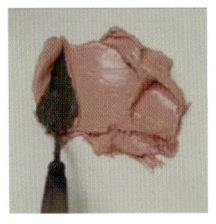

Impasto (left): The surface texture of a work of art.

Impressionism (below): A loose, spontaneous style of painting that originated in France circa 1870. The style is characterized by the use of pure (often unmixed) colors and short brushstrokes.

Intaglio: A printing process in which the image is incised or etched into a metal plate using a variety of methods and tools. Etching, engraving, aquatint, mezzotint and drypoint are common intaglio techniques.

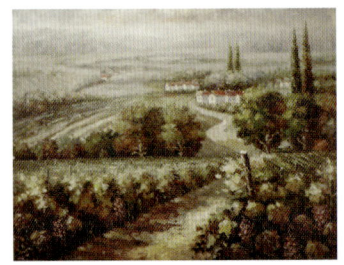

"Tuscan View" by unknown artist.

Landscape: A painting, drawing or photograph which depicts outdoor scenery. Typically includes trees, streams, buildings, crops, mountains, wildlife, rivers and forests.

Light Damage: Can alter chemicals in paper and paint, and cause a composition's colors to fade. The extent of the damage from ultraviolet light (sunlight) depends on intensity and length of exposure.

Limited Edition: A limit placed on the number of prints produced in a particular edition, in order to create a scarcity. Usually each print is numbered sequentially followed by the total edition size (i.e. 1/250).

Linocut: An abbreviation of linoleum cut. Similar to a woodcut, but with variations owing to the relatively soft properties of linoleum.

Listed Artist: A term commonly used by appraisers to describe artists 'listed' in standard art reference books.

Lithography: The process of printing from a flat surface treated so as to repel the ink except where it is required for printing. Operates on the principle that oil and water don't mix.

Lost Wax: A method of bronze casting using a clay core and a wax coating placed in a mold. The wax is melted in the mold, drained, and bronze poured into the hollow area, producing a bronze composition when the core is discarded.

Medium/Media: Material or technique an artist works in; also, the component of paint in which the pigment is dispersed.

Mezzotint: A printmaking process of the intaglio family that allows for tones and shading to be produced without line or dot-based techniques like hatching, cross-hatching or stipple.

Middle Tier/Mid-Tier: For the purpose of this book, refers to artists that, while not household names, have established a reputation for their art through prestigious awards, exhibitions, and sales.

Mint Condition: An expression used in the description of pre-owned goods. Originally referred to the condition of coins, but now commonly used to describe any item having excellent, like-new quality.

Monogram: A combination of letters, usually initials, used in place of a traditional signature on an artwork.

Monoprint: A unique, single impression of an image made from a reprintable block.

Mount: A protective backing that a print or drawing is affixed to.

Museum: A building or institution devoted to the acquisition, conservation, study, exhibition and educational interpretation of objects having scientific, historical or artistic value.

Offset Lithography: A four-color printing technique that uses inks, carried by rubber rollers called printing blankets, to transfer photographed images from metal plates to paper.

Oil: A type of paint made from color particles (pigment) and linseed oil. Dries slowly, can be applied in thick or thin layers, and with or without glazes.

Open Edition: A series of prints or objects in an art edition that has an unlimited number of copies.

Original: Implies exclusivity or that the work is 'one of a kind' rather than a mechanically reproduced copy. Entails direct involvement by the original artist in its creation and production.

Overpaint: The painting over of original areas of a composition during restoration.

Palette: Refers to the instrument used to hold the paint in painting, as well as the range of colors used by a particular artist.

Palette Knife: A tool used in mixing paint on a palette, and utilized to spread paint thickly like butter on a canvas or other support material.

Pastel: A stick consisting of chalk pigment mixed with water-based binding material.

Patina: A film produced by oxidation on the surface of metals. It is often esteemed for its ornamental value and may be artificially applied (for aesthetic reasons) by the artist or craftsman.

Perspective: The art of picturing objects on a flat surface so as to give the appearance of distance or depth.

Photogravure: An intaglio process where printing is done from a plate in which a photographic negative has been transferred and etched.

Plate: The plate is the printing element (usually metal), on which an intaglio, relief or planographic process is employed.

Plate Mark: An indentation in paper caused by the pressure of the plate against it during the intaglio printing process.

Plate-Signed: Prints in which the artist's signature, as it appears in the original work, is put onto the reproduction plate and transferred to the print through the same process as the rest of the design.

Plein Air: French for "open air." Refers to landscapes and seascapes painted on-site, in real time, without aid of photography.

Point of View: The position from which something is seen or considered (i.e., head-on, overhead, ground level, etc.).

Portraiture: The art or practice of making portraits.

Print: A design or picture transferred from a plate, block, lithographic stone, or other medium.

Proof: A sample print utilized for quality control prior to its full production.

Provenance: The known history of an artwork.

Publisher's Proof (P/P): A special edition of a print published for the publisher's personal inspection, use, and possible sale.

Rag Mat: Used in conservational framing, rag matting is constructed of acid-free cotton fibers.

Realism/Realistic (right): A style of painting which depicts subject matter (form, color, space) as it appears naturally without distortion or stylization. Sometimes called "photorealism."

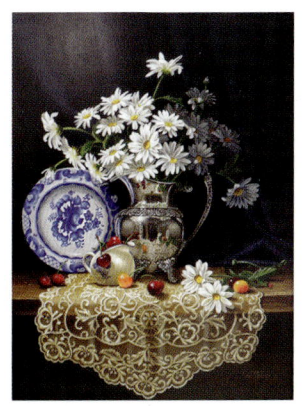

"Vintage Lace"
by Luba Stolper.

Recast: Refers to previously cast sculptures in which the mold used in the casting process is taken from an existing bronze. This results in a degradation of the composition.

Recto: The front of a two-dimensional object.

Relief: Block printing technique in which the raised areas are inked and provide the color of a print. (*Please Note: This is the opposite of Intaglio printing where the incised areas are inked.*) Woodcuts and linocuts are two common examples of relief printing.

Reproduction: A recreation that imitates the form and elements of an original work.

Remarque: A small sketch or watercolor, usually handmade by the artist, which may accompany a special fine art edition.

Restoration: Repair of artwork with the aim to correct damage caused by improper handling, exposure to the elements, or any other destructive force.

Screen Print: See Serigraph.

Sculpture: Any three-dimensional form created as an artistic expression.

Seascape: A painting or work of art that depicts the sea or a scene that includes the sea.

Secondary Market: The resale market for previously owned artwork. Primarily refers to the market created when prints are sold out at the publisher. Prices are then determined by the process of supply and demand.

Serigraph: A print made using a stencil process in which a design is superimposed on a silk screen, and printing ink is squeegeed through the area of the screen not covered by the stencil.

Shill(s): Phony bidders employed at auctions in order to drive up prices and provoke a bidding war among other participants.

Silk Screen: See Serigraph.

Signed and Numbered: See Limited Edition.

Sketch: A rough drawing used to capture the basic elements and structure of a situation often used as the basis for a more detailed work.

Starving Artist: Someone who sacrifices material well-being in order to focus on their art.

Stone Lithography: A printing technique in which an image is drawn on a stone (usually limestone) by the artist, in reverse, and then pressed onto paper or canvas.

Support: The physical structure that holds an artwork's media. This can be any material—such as wood, metal, canvas or paper—on which a work of art is executed.

Surrealism: A style of art developed in Europe during the 1920s. Surrealism is characterized by the utilization of the subconscious as a source of creativity, and often depicts unexpected or irrational objects. Salvador Dali (right) was a major proponent of the style.

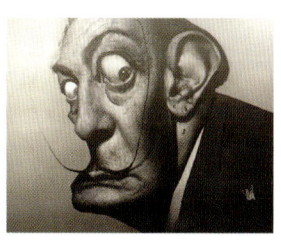

"The Persistence of Dali" by Jota Leal.

UV (Ultraviolet) Glass: Specially filtered glass that blocks the majority of harmful Ultraviolet light.

Varnish: A thin protective coating applied to a painting. There are natural and synthetic varnishes.

Verso: The reverse or back of a two-dimensional object.

Watercolor: A water-based paint that is transparent.

Woodblock: See Woodcut.

Woodcut: A method of relief printing in which wood is the printing element.

About the Author

Brett K. Maly has served as Director for *Art encounter* for nearly twenty years and has a wide breadth of knowledge in all manner of fine art. Certified as an appraiser through the University of California at Irvine's Certification Program in Fine and Decorative Arts, Mr. Maly is a member of the American Society of Appraisers and is certified in the Uniform Standards of Professional Appraisal Practice (USPAP).

In addition to appraising fine art for collectors and institutions, Mr. Maly has appeared as an expert on radio and television, including his recurring role as the art expert for The History Channel's internationally syndicated show, Pawn Stars, where he has discussed everything from fine art valuation, to its collection and preservation.

The majority of artworks photographed in this text are available for purchase. To inquire, please call the offices of *Art encounter* 702-227-0220.
